YOUR KINGDOM COME

*Experience the Glory and
Beauty of God's Kingdom!
Right here! Right now!*

ALEC N. CAPAY

WESTBOW
PRESS®
A DIVISION OF THOMAS NELSON
& ZONDERVAN

This book is a work of non-fiction. Unless otherwise noted, the author and the publisher make no explicit guarantees as to the accuracy of the information contained in this book and in some cases, names of people and places have been altered to protect their privacy.

Scripture quotes marked (KJV) are taken from the King James Version of the Bible.

Scripture quotations marked (NIV) are taken from the Holy Bible, New International Version®, NIV®. Copyright © 1973, 1978, 1984, 2011 by Biblica, Inc.™ Used by permission of Zondervan. All rights reserved worldwide.

Scripture quotations taken from the New American Standard Bible® (NASB), Copyright © 1960, 1962, 1963, 1968, 1971, 1972, 1973, 1975, 1977, 1995 by The Lockman Foundation.Used by permission. www.Lockman.org

WestBow Press books may be ordered through booksellers or by contacting:

WestBow Press
A Division of Thomas Nelson & Zondervan
1663 Liberty Drive
Bloomington, IN 47403
www.westbowpress.com
1 (866) 928-1240

Because of the dynamic nature of the Internet, any web addresses or links contained in this book may have changed since publication and may no longer be valid. The views expressed in this work are solely those of the author and do not necessarily reflect the views of the publisher, and the publisher hereby disclaims any responsibility for them.

Any people depicted in stock imagery provided by Thinkstock are models, and such images are being used for illustrative purposes only. Certain stock imagery © Thinkstock.

ISBN: 978-1-5127-7499-3 (sc)
ISBN: 978-1-5127-7500-6 (e)

Print information available on the last page.

WestBow Press rev. date: 02/06/2017

Then the King will say to those on His right hand,
'Come, you blessed of My Father, inherit the kingdom
prepared for you from the foundation of the world.'
Matthew 25:34

CONTENTS

Acknowledgements...ix
Prologue..xi
Introduction...xiii

Chapter 1   What is the Kingdom?......................................1
Chapter 2   Present or Future Kingdom? 9
Chapter 3   Kingdom Responsibilities & Mandate 19
Chapter 4   The Gospel of the Kingdom............................29
Chapter 5   Kingdom Advancement 39
Chapter 6   The Citizen 49
Chapter 7   Seeking His Kingdom....................................65
Chapter 8   The Kingdom Now 71

Bibliography..77
About the Author 81

ACKNOWLEDGEMENTS

To my family who have supported me throughout the years. Your continued support and encouragement have made it possible for me to pursue my passion to write. There are not enough words to express my gratitude.

To the Senior pastors of Faith Alive Family Church, Brent and Barb Rudoski. There are a few who can carry the title of heroes of the faith. These are such people. It's your life I salute and honor.

To my dear mother, Sarah. I want to acknowledge your incredible strength of character and love. Despite the many times of despair and tragedy, you continued to clutch hold to the nail-scarred hand of the crucified Lamb. Where would I be without you? Since the day you placed a Bible in my hands and made that bold proclamation, *"Here you go, son! Now preach from it!"* From that time, I have continued to preach that same gospel. You stood strong in faith where others could not. All that I am, I am because of your love and prayers.

Val, you are the best! I couldn't have done it without you! Thank you for the long hours of editing and proofreading.

Last and definitely not least, to my beautiful wife, Kareen. There is so much to thank you for that these pages could not contain it all. I would never have made it this far without you. Your support of this book and during my most trying times have been amazing. Your testimony of faithfulness has shown me what it means to serve God with an undivided heart. To me, you will always be the greatest Christian.

PROLOGUE

Never in my imagination had I ever thought about writing on such a broad topic. Having studied on this subject for several years, it feels as though I've just scratched the surface. I am convinced the Kingdom of God is the entire culmination of all that He is and does. There is so much more on this subject about the Kingdom of God than what is compiled in this book. It is such a wonderful subject to read about. During my studies, I've discovered the richness from the Word and other sources when it comes to understanding the different concepts regarding kings and a kingdom. One cannot describe or illustrate the Kingdom of God to one book.

Yet in the midst of all of this, I've often wondered and asked: how could a young Native boy reach such a prestigious point in his life? Even after having graduated Bible College with a Masters Degree in Theology and writing two books, this is a question I have often asked myself again and again. Growing up on a First Nation reservation had its ups and downs. I didn't know what it was like to live in an urban setting. We had been slightly isolated for several years and had to make a few trips a year to nearest town just to buy needed supplies. If and when my family weren't able to afford the things we needed, we lived off the land.

I was fortunate to be raised on a reservation where we were not oppressed. We lived as though nothing could ever touch us or reach us. I am thankful for my heritage and culture. I will never regret being raised on a reservation but I began to think of the opportunities I could attained as I looked beyond the borders of my home community.

What happened? I believed there was a world waiting for me. I had to make a choice that there was more than just living in the confides of my home community. Is growing up on a reserve wrong? Absolutely not! Yes, in many reservations, we have problems of suicide, teenage pregnancy, and many others. A majority of people would search online for information and statistics to receive answers, but life on the reservation is an entirely different experience in itself.

Why would I share my story at the beginning of this book? I've never been one to settle for the mediocre. I've done my best to dedicate myself fully to everything that I do because when I set out to do something, I don't know how to do it with anything less than with all of my heart. But often times, this projects me into places where I feel completely overwhelmed, worn out, and even lost. However, without the help of my family and friends, my church and pastors, my wife and son, and most of all, Jesus Christ, I would not have been where I am today. I refused to put myself in a position where I felt insignificant. You might think to yourself that you are one insignificant person living on this planet, feeling like you're just about to be swept in the everyday rush of this world, but you have to make up your mind and stop allowing people and circumstances around you dictate and overpower you. As I've always said and believed: this life is not a destination but a journey. Enjoy it!

Alec N. Capay
Saskatoon, Saskatchewan

INTRODUCTION

...all the elders of Israel gathered themselves together, and came to Samuel unto Ramah, And said unto him, Behold, thou art old, and thy sons walk in thy ways: now make us a king to judge us like all the nations. (1 Samuel 8:4,5)

Can you imagine how the heart of God felt? Here are a people, whose history is filled with supernatural events; from the plagues in Egypt to the parting of the Red Sea, from the walls of Jericho being demolished to quail and manna coming down from heaven. However, the children of Israel grew tired and dissatisfied with God as their king. They approached the prophet Samuel and submitted their request. The Bible tells us, *"The thing displeased Samuel..."* (1 Samuel 8:6). In the following verse, God spoke to Samuel and said, *"...they have not rejected thee, but they have rejected me, that I should not reign over them"* (1Samuel 8:7).

The *IVP Bible Background Commentary on the Old Testament*, it says,

> *The leaders of Israel have decided they want a permanent head of government empowered with centralized authority over the tribes and commanding a standing army. They have concluded that their organization as a federation of tribes has put them at a military disadvantage. They*

believe that a king with a trained standing army at his command will level the playing field and enable them to successfully defend their land. They have been mistaken in assessing their problem as a political problem and consequently opting for a political solution. What Samuel seeks to clarify for them is that their problem is not political but spiritual. Their political solution will solve nothing unless it is accompanied by a spiritual solution.

We have to remember that in the progression of leadership throughout Israel's history there was never a passing of the mantle of authority onto the next generation of leaders. *"...and there arose another generation after them, which knew not the Lord, nor yet the works which he had done for Israel"* (Judges 2:10). Up until this point, God was their sovereign leader and King. Yes, Moses and Joshua served as Israel's leaders through the times of the wilderness, but then the children of Israel had this unwarranted desire of wanting a king like all the other nations around them. However, this did not take God by surprise. He knew very well that there would be a long line of kings in the days to come in the nation of Israel.

The motivation behind Israel's request was not pure. They wanted to be like other nations. Yes, God wanted to eventually establish kings, but the time was not yet. He already had a kingdom established on earth. The request displeased Samuel and God. The children of Israel were not ready for a physical king at that point. They had just gone through the wilderness for 40 years and there was a trust issue that needed to be resolved and restored. They had to learn to trust in the Lord again to lead them as their king.

Why am I saying all this? The very same is applicable to us today as believers in Jesus. Yes, we are part of the Kingdom of God, yet we can run the risk of seeking the kingdom more than the King Himself. In his lecture on *The Kingdom of God*, J.D. King puts it, *"God called Himself a king, something the people would have understood, but God would help His people understand that His purpose and plans were greater than the feeble reach of the earthly sovereigns."* He wanted to tell His people that

He was King of not only of a particular group or nation but over all the earth. Even though Israel was appointed a king, Saul, this man was still appointed and anointed by God and His prophet to lead the children of Israel. In later years, God continued to establish kings in the land of Israel. We find that God had a plan with the ideas of kings and kingdom. It is amazing to me that we know nothing or very little about the concepts of a kingdom and a king.

A Different Picture

As a child, I heard the Kingdom of God referenced through the Parables of Jesus. The teacher would tell the story and start out with something like, *"The Kingdom of God is like..."* Yet in all my years as a child, I never understood the concept as the different messages would speak of a certain people or illustrate a particular event. Most of the parables I heard as a child sounded like stories, but I never realized that each parable held a powerful truth regarding Jesus and His Kingdom. I would often see framed pictures hanging on my parents walls, or at the local Christian bookstore, portraying clouds in the sky carrying a bright city, with castle-like buildings and houses. This was a picture I had in my mind as a young boy when thinking about the Kingdom of God. Most of the time I would think to myself, *"I wonder what it would be like to go this place."* This was the image I had in my mind when I thought about the Kingdom of God.

What Changed?

I'm sure most of you are wondering the same thing, especially as we entered into a new millennium in human history. What is God doing? What is He up to?

We cannot draw any conclusions when it comes to understanding and knowing about the Kingdom of God. It is a very broad subject and we may never grasp its full meaning. Jesus said, *"The kingdom of heaven (God) is like a mustard seed..."* (Matthew 13:31). There are volumes upon volumes of books written on the Kingdom of God, yet each one is like a mustard seed. This writing is nothing but a small mustard seed, which will grow in time in future writings.

> *The King will say to those on His right side, 'Come, you who are blessed by my Father, take your inheritance, the kingdom prepared for you since the creation of the world.'*
> (Matthew 25:34)

I invite you to join me on this wonderful journey as we examine the Scriptures, visit ancient customs, and first-century cultural beliefs that will help set the stage for God's plan and purpose for people like you and I. God has bestowed upon the Body of Christ something amazing, and everyone can gain access to if we welcome it. It's called the Kingdom of God. He has given us these spiritual truths to serve as a compass to help guide us in this journey called life.

CHAPTER 1

What is the Kingdom?

As I take a stroll down memory lane, my mind goes back to the sandy roads of my home reservation in the backwoods of Northwestern Ontario. I can almost hear the whistling through the trees and the roaring sound of a motorized boat passing by. I remember sitting, summer after summer, listening to Bible lessons, stories, and hearing songs such as, *"Obedience is the very best way to show that you believe. Doing exactly what the Lord commands, doing it happily."* During those impressionable years, I was fascinated with sermons preached by prominent Aboriginal ministers who brought forth the Word with simplicity and power. The ministering and singing of old songs such as, *"Years I spent in vanity and pride, caring not my Lord was crucified, Knowing not it was for me He died, at Calvary,"* all made a lasting imprint on my mind. Through it all, my heart and mind had never been given a clear explanation of the Kingdom of God. It was taught in those days that it was a place where we will go to someday, not realizing it was something we can experience now. However, I am and will always be truly grateful for my spiritual heritage and to all those that brought me to the saving knowledge of Jesus Christ.

Several years later, I was given the opportunity to attend a Pentecostal Bible College in the prairies of Central Canada. After three years of study, I graduated successfully and earned a Diploma in Theology, but the stirring interest in spiritual things remained unsettled during this time. My only recollection of the Kingdom of God was found in what many of us are familiar with, the "Lord's Prayer" that reads, *"Our Father, which art in heaven, Hallowed be thy Name. Thy Kingdom come, Thy will be done in earth, as it is in heaven"* (Matthew 6:9,10). Little did I realize,*"The Kingdom of God is like a treasure hid in a field, the which when a man hath found, he hideth, and for joy thereof he goeth and selleth all that he hath, and buyeth that field"* (Matthew 13:44). After being in ministry following graduation from Bible College, I still found myself on a journey to discover what the Kingdom of God was all about and how it could apply to my everyday life.

My wife and I moved to Central Canada and attended a church that had a Bible training centre as one of its affiliate ministries. It was one simple statement during a class that gave me a greater desire to know and study the Kingdom of God further. The statement went something like this, *"The Kingdom of God is God's way of doing things."* Since then, I've been on a journey to know and understand the Kingdom of God, and hopefully, I can make some sense in this book.

In our Western culture, we are unfamiliar with the concept of *Kingdom* because we live a democratic society in which power is vested in the people, who rule either directly or through freely elected representatives. Therefore, we generally have no concept of what being in a kingdom means. When we think of the term *kingdom*, we often associate it with the United Kingdom or some medieval past that consisted of a monarch, lords, castles, armies, and so on. When we gain an understanding of the concepts of a kingdom, we can better understand the Bible, God, and His plans and purposes. When we begin to understand the concept of kingdom, the better we will understand God and His ways.

During biblical times, it was common to use the word, *kingdom*. Jesus used this terminology several times in His teachings of the parables. Throughout the entirety of that region, from its towns to it citizens, it was ruled and dominated by a kingdom and a king. The Roman Empire was the ruling power during the time of Jesus. Its dominance and force stretched from England to Africa, and from Syria to Spain. In almost every region under Roman rule, an average of one in four people died by the dictatorship of Roman law and government. It is not surprising that much of Roman influence consisted of mixed sophistication, bridled with brutality and tyranny. Because of such atrocities, the entire Roman Empire was known for it terror, tyranny, and tenacity.

This would leave us with little surprise that Jesus entered into a generation of people that knew the concept of a king and kingdom. In fact, during this time, Jesus illustrated much of His teaching with the current surroundings and environment and ways in which His hearers would understand. Unfortunately, much of the religious sector claiming to know the Hebrew God had very little knowledge about these concepts. Walter A. Elwell shares further details concerning the Kingdom of God, *"The heart of Jesus' teachings centers around the theme of the kingdom of God. This expression is found in the sixty-one separate sayings in the Synoptic Gospels."* However, in their minds, the Messiah which was prophesied about was to establish a David-like kingdom in Jerusalem. Upon the establishment of this kingdom, Jesus would then free Israel from Roman dictatorship. Was this the reason why Jesus brought the Kingdom? After Jesus was considered as a political revolutionary, when He came riding in on Palm Sunday and hailed as a king, and gathered to Himself a group of men. We will discuss this further in the chapters following.

No Kingdom without a King

We must understand that without a king, there can be no kingdom. All of Rome was under the strong rule of these different Emperors, which they called Caesars. As history records, some ruled with an iron fist accompanied with savagery and cruelty, yet there were others who ruled with fine qualities and character. In our western mentality, we have no concept of the word, king, because we are governed by a President or a Prime Minister. We also have elected officials, such as Ministers of Parliament, Congress, Judges, National Grand Chief, Deputy Grand Chiefs, Mayors, Council Members, and so on. However, when we think of the position of a king, we often think of a throne, a crown, a golden scepter, along with subject and lords, etc. We have also seen several versions of kings depicted in Hollywood movies or graphic novels. My good friend, Adam Biro, in his book, *Kingdom of Priests*, said it this way, *"Pop culture paints a superficial picture of what a kingdom should look like. Our Disney-vision of a castle on a hill, a noble king, and charming prince pervades our subconscious thought. A kingdom is a land far, far away filled with mystery and adventure. The heroes of the kingdom are knights in shining armour. Its villains are witches, dragons and so forth. Like it or not, we must admit that these are images that flood our imaginations."* It is a lightweight version of the concept of a king and his kingdom. Throughout the history of man, and especially in the eastern part of the world, its citizens have been under the rule of kings and kingdoms. In the Western world, things have drastically changed with democracy playing a primary role in shaping civilization, in the way we act, think, and even govern. There are possibly millions of people who would shrink back as they begin to hear terminology such as this. We may find ourselves to be intimidated by these usage of words.

What Changed?

In 1776, the United States of America claimed independence from the sovereign rule of Britain and therefore, democracy was born. In Philadelphia, Pennsylvania, the Declaration of Independence was written and the United States, with its thirteen newly independent, sovereign states, was no longer part of the British Empire. They declared, in some form, a rebellion against a king and a kingdom and were no longer under the sovereign rule of Great Britain. America no longer saw the need for a king nor remain under a kingdom.

We also have to be careful when we mention the word, *kingdom* to the people around us. For instance, we have another religious organization called, *Jehovah's Witnesses,* which was founded by the late Charles Taze Russell. They have the belief that destruction is imminent for this present world through Armageddon, and that God is going to establish His Kingdom as the only solution to all the problems of humanity. Many of you have probably noticed on their buildings or meeting houses, a sign that says, *Kingdom Hall.* We must not confuse ourselves with the concepts and beliefs of the Jehovah's Witnesses and think that's what Jesus taught in the Gospels about the Kingdom.

The late Dr. Myles Munroe, in his book, *Rediscovering the Kingdom,* said, *"If you do not understand kingdoms, it is impossible for you to understand the Bible and its messages."* He continues, *"...over the past 2,000 years the concept of the kingdom has been lost, especially since the advent of modern governments built on new concepts of governing, democracy, socialism, communism, and dictatorship."* With our lack of understanding regarding these concepts, we can never really understand the plan and purposes of God. How can we call Him *King Jesus* without understanding the role and position of a king? How can we label ourselves as a royal priesthood, as Peter describes it, if we do not familiarize ourselves with the concepts of royalty or monarchy?

Making a Shift

How could we overlook such a central theme in the message of Jesus? The church has focused on so many different doctrines and beliefs through the centuries, such as healing, miracles, salvation, discipleship, missions, evangelism, the Holy Spirit, etc. There is nothing wrong with any of these doctrines, but have we missed the central message of Jesus? Unfortunately, the Kingdom of God has not been the central truth or theme, nor has it taken prominence in many churches and Bible schools. There exists a gulf between modern day theology and that which Jesus taught during His earthly ministry. As we read the accounts of Jesus in the gospels, we would be surprised of how much the term Kingdom of God is used. So why don't we use it and define it in greater detail in our sermons? I would submit to you that our understanding of the Kingdom is very limited.

Before we can make a shift in our thinking and attitude towards the Kingdom, we must first understand what the Kingdom is. How do we define the Kingdom? First of all, we must understand that a kingdom has a culture. What is a culture? A culture is a way of life. It is a group of people who operate through certain behaviours, beliefs, values, and symbols. For most cultures, many of these practices are not thought through but are practiced without even thinking about it. Most cultural acts and behaviours are done naturally. These are mainly passed along by communication and imitation from one generation to the next. Examples of different cultural groups and practices can be seen everywhere around us.

First of all, we have Pop Culture. It is not necessarily defined as Pop Culture, but Popular Culture. It is simply the activities of the people in a particular country. It is generated by what they listen to, what they read, what they wear, and how they speak. It is unfortunate that most of our English words have been distorted over the years. For example, at one time in history, the word "gay" referred to someone who was happy or excited. Now it has been interpreted as someone who is attracted to a person of the same sex.

Secondly, particular best-selling books and popular films can play a significant role in shaping the opinions and experiences of our culture. Many have been shaped by the latest trends in music by their favorite artists who may include those on the Billboard Top 100 or from the latest song on YouTube. The way we interact and socialize has drastically changed.

Thirdly, through the advancement of technology, social networking has provided a vehicle for us to communicate with family and friends at any time or place. We have come a long way since Alexander Graham Bell developed his method of communication through the telephone. What kind of world would we be living in if it had not been for his invention? We also have to consider the Internet and the World Wide Web, which play a significant part in our communication with one another, and also contribute to the passing and gathering of information between households, companies, schools, and businesses. It has far surpassed television, radio, and the newspaper.

Lastly, we have the culture of fashion. It is amazing to see how fashion has evolved over the decades and how it has influenced and changed the way people feel about themselves. There was a time in history when certain cultural groups were only allowed to wear a particular type of clothing. In today's society, it is reflected by the mood they are in or what is being showcased in the media as the latest style of clothing.

It is wonderful to imagine how far along we have come as a culture, especially in North America. But what of the Kingdom of God? How do we relate the Kingdom of God to a culture? First, a kingdom can and must have influence over its citizens and cause an impact in their lives. Also, that same culture and influence must be reflected and expressed through its citizens. Secondly, we have to understand that a king has a mind, a will, and a purpose. When we think of the passage in Matthew 6:10, *"Your kingdom come...,"* how is the mind of the King, along with His will and purpose, going to influence and impact in the world today? Through its citizens. It must be a collective design of the mind and spirit of each citizen.

When we think of the term, *culture*, we must also include the term, *"colony."* What is a colony? A colony is a group of people who settle in a new place but keep ties to their homeland. It is also a territory that is ruled from a distance by a kingdom, and that same kingdom impacts the colony with its culture until it looks, behaves, and characterizes itself like the kingdom that it is subject to. What happens in the kingdom should manifest in the colony.

We are going to discover in the next few chapters what the culture of the Kingdom of God consists of. It is vitally important that we learn about and study the different types of cultures in the world today, especially those that operate through a monarch or kingdom mentality. It will help us gain a better understanding of God's Kingdom so that we may better appreciate His ways and values.

CHAPTER 2

Present or Future Kingdom?

I t is my hope that you don't get confused with the idea of God's future Kingdom and His Kingdom now. Whatever your belief is regarding the future of the world and the church, I hope to emphasize an important truth and do justice to what I'm about to say. Yes, God has a future Kingdom in mind and a place where He makes His habitation. He also has a longing to establish His Kingdom here on planet Earth, which He desired from the foundations of the world. More importantly, He's already begun to establish His Kingdom on Earth.

As a young man growing up, I listened to different ministers preach messages about the rapture and the end times. Some years later, I heard the fancy theological term – eschatology. I will admit, during my first few years of preaching the gospel, I preached messages liked I'd heard. I even sang about the coming of Jesus, the rapture, etc. I stormed up and down the platform, warning people in the congregation that there is coming a day, soon and very soon when we shall see the King. I grew up hearing songs from the old hymn book that said, *"Some glad morning when this life is O'er, I'll fly away,"* or *"There's a blessed time that's coming, coming soon! It may be evening, morning, or at noon."* Every so often, I would hear the simple message preached, *"Wouldn't it be wonderful if we all got raptured today before we got out of this building?"* Many have used, in their preaching, the *Left Behind* or *Get Right or Get Left* method. Again, I am not degrading these ministers and ministries. I love them as brothers and sisters in the Lord. I do not doubt the intent and motivation of these ministers. I believe them to be pure and carried with a good heart. In fact I am very proud of my Christian heritage and where I came from. However, there is a bigger picture to look at if we are ever going to understand the Kingdom of God.

I want to spend this section on this topic because it is essential for us to understand, first of all, where we are today. It will help us understand what we will be reading in the next few chapters. In the book of Matthew, we have a man, a prophet, a voice crying in the wilderness – John the Baptist. As John said in his account, *"There was a man sent from God whose name was John..."* (John 1:6). John came with a message of repentance and of the Kingdom. Matthew records, *"In those days John the Baptist, preaching in the wilderness of Judea. And saying, Repent! For the kingdom of heaven is at hand"* (Matthew 3:1-2)! We have to keep in mind that John carried an important responsibility, and that was to open the door and prepare the way for the Lord come. Jesus said of John, *"I tell you the truth: Among those born of women there has not risen anyone greater than John the Baptist; yet he who is least in the kingdom of heaven is greater than he"* (Matthew 11:11). It is amazing that the first declaration of John was the Kingdom of God as it was the message of Jesus. Accompanying John's proclamation of the Kingdom was repentance. What is repentance? And how does it tie into the message of the Kingdom? Many of us know that repentance means, *"a complete change of mind and thinking – a whole new mentality – and a complete change of direction."* This is how we understand repentance. But how can we tie this into the Kingdom? To gain access to His Kingdom, we must repent, change our thinking, our mentality, and our direction.

We have to keep in mind that the majority of people whom Jesus and John were speaking to, were Jewish men and women. They knew the Scriptures and had an in-depth knowledge of the things of God. Their audience were not pagans or unbelievers. We would be surprised that most of the people whom Jesus spoke to were believers in Yahweh. This is primarily the reason why Jesus and John exhorted them to repent. They had to change their minds about certain thing and gain a whole new mentality and direction.

Shortly after the baptism of Jesus and following the temptation in the wilderness, He began His public ministry, *"From that time Jesus began to preach and to say, Repent: for the kingdom of heaven is at hand"* (Matthew 4:17). What were Jesus and John speaking of when they said the words, *is at hand*?

When Jesus came preaching and announcing the Kingdom of heaven is at hand, He was saying it is within reach. It is here! The *New American Standard Bible* says, *"...the kingdom of heaven has come near."* From then on, Jesus began to demonstrate the Kingdom of God by healing the sick, performing miracles, casting out devils, and commanding nature. The Bible says: *"And His fame went throughout all Syria: and they brought unto Him all sick people that were taken with divers diseases and torments, and those which were possessed with devils, and those which were lunatic, and those that had the palsy; and He healed them"* (Matthew 4:24). Jesus also said in the book of Luke, *"But if I am casting out demons by the power of God, then the Kingdom of God has arrived among you"* (Luke 11:20). We have seen through Scripture that the Kingdom is not in the far future, but an experience we can attain today. Unfortunately, modern day theology have relegated the kingdom of God to a future time and date.

In My Father's House...Many Mansions

In my Father's house there are many mansions: if it were not so, I would have told you, I go to prepare a place for you. And if I go and prepare a place for you, I will come again, and receive you unto myself: that where I am, there ye may be also. (John 14:2)

Most of you have, at one time, heard this passage of Scripture used during a funeral service. The classic sermon would refer to the deceased as receiving a mansion in heaven when passing from this life over into the next. Of course, to the average reader, this sounds very self-explanatory, and many have taken it literally. We have painted a picture in our minds of Jesus in heaven with a tool belt around His waist building all these mansions and probably having to do it very quickly because He could be sent back to Earth at any moment. But, unless we grasp what the writer was explaining, we run the risk of missing out on what Jesus was referring to. Craig S. Keener said,

> *The "Father's House" would be the temple where God would forever dwell with His people. The "dwelling places" could allude to the booths constructed for the Feast of Tabernacles but probably refer to "rooms" in the new temple, where only undefiled ministers would have a place. John presumably means this language figuratively for being in Christ, where God's presence dwells.*

Many ministers in New Testament times would come from different regions around Jerusalem. When a visiting minister comes to our local church, we usually book a hotel room where he or she can stay comfortably during their visit. However, in the temple complex, small rooms were constructed for different ministers coming to visit during an annual feast or for a particular event on the Jewish calendar. When Jesus said, *"In my Father's house, there are many mansions...,"* He was saying, in my Father's house (temple), there are many rooms. Jesus also spoke of preparation because He was preparing a place of ministry for His disciples, who were, at that time, observing the miracles and healing, and the casting out of demons. He said, *"...that where I am, there you may be also."* Jesus was implying that where I am, healing the sick, performing miracles, and casting out demons, there you may be also. He wanted His disciples to walk in that same demonstration of Kingdom power and authority, and He wants us, as believers today, to walk in as well. Jesus said later, in that same chapter, *"...the works that I do shall he do also, and greater works than these shall he do; because I go unto my Father"* (John 14:12). The Kingdom of God is at hand! Don't miss it!

It is a tragic situation when followers of Jesus believe that the Kingdom of God is beyond the scope of human reach. Why is this?

I would submit to you that many of these ideas stem from the belief that Jesus is coming soon. During the late eighteen and early nineteen hundreds, the concept of the *rapture* adopted a mentality that world evangelization should not be the chief aim, but the only aim of God's people. During this time, there was a man by the name of John Nelson Darby, who believed that the rapture would soon take place and that the true church should not be involved in secular affairs. In fact, William DeArteaga quotes Darby, he said, *"There was no time for the church to concern itself with social issues or even to teach the disciplines of the Christian faith."* To our surprise, much of Darby's ideas trickled into many North American churches, where they produced a mentality of "what's the use!" I have heard reports of certain individuals refusing to marry, parents forbidding their children to attend university or college, and also those who let their horses run wild and free so that they wouldn't starve to death because the time was so close. Am I denouncing the rapture of the church? Am I degrading this belief that has permeated the minds of so many North Americans? Absolutely not! I believe Jesus is coming back, but it may not necessarily be constructed in the fashion that so many in the church believe today. It is not even a question of when He is coming, but rather, why is He coming back?

In order for us to truly understand Jesus' mission and purpose, we first understand why He came in the flesh first of all. Are we in fact blind today as those religious leaders of Jesus' time? When the Kingdom of God came, not only in Word, but also in demonstration, they missed it or did not recognize it. Are we as guilty of missing the Kingdom today? We must understand that when Jesus came, the Kingdom came with Him, and we no longer have to anticipate His Kingdom in the future. It has invaded our present.

Pastor Steve Gray, in his book, *When the Kingdom Comes*, said, *"For centuries the Jews had expected the Kingdom to come to them. Their expectation rested on a King David type of king and an Elijah type of Messiah who would defeat all Israel's oppressors and, through the Jews, rule the earth."* It is true that many Jewish people believed He came, but not in the way they wanted. Much of the traditional Jewish community believe He has not yet arrived and are still in waiting for the Messiah. I can almost imagine the reaction of those religious Jews. Here was Jesus, born in a manger, wrapped in swaddling clothes, and surrounded by sheep and cows.

More Than a Christmas Story

For unto us a child is born, unto us a son is given: and the government shall be upon his shoulders: and his name shall be called Wonderful, Counsellor, The mighty God, The everlasting Father, The Prince of Peace. Of the increase of his government there shall be no end, upon the throne of David, and upon his kingdom, to order it, and to establish it with judgment and with justice from henceforth even for ever. The zeal of the Lord of hosts will perform this. (Isaiah 9:6,7)

When we read these passages, our minds automatically revert to the Christmas story and the birth of Jesus. At first glance, these verses speak of a child being born. However, to the Jews, this speaks of the ideal king that would sit upon the throne of David. This brings me back to the time when Jesus was handed the scroll of Isaiah, the prophet during the reading of Scripture in the synagogue. We find this story in Luke 4:16-20. *"The Spirit of the Lord is upon me..."* (Luke 4:18). Immediately after reading the portion from Isaiah, Jesus handed the scroll back to the minister and went and sat down. Why is this important? It is believed that a seat in the synagogue was reserved for the Messiah, of which He will take occupancy. This is a different study within itself. As mentioned earlier, many of the Jewish believers in Jesus' time believed the Messiah would come with power and great glory, and as a warrior who would overthrow the Roman government. When Jesus was born, it was in a manger surrounded by sheep, cows, and visited by shepherds. It was an unlikely place for a king to be born. How could this be the Messiah? Little did the religious leaders realize, they would be fulfilling Isaiah's prophecy in Isaiah 53:3-12.

*He was despised and rejected of men; a man of sorrows,
and acquainted with grief...Surely he hath borne our griefs
and carried our sorrows: yet we did esteem him stricken,
smitten of God, and afflicted...He was oppressed, and he
was afflicted, yet he opened not his mouth: he is brought
as a lamb to the slaughter...He was taken from prison
and from judgment...He made his grave with the wicked,
and with the rich in his death; because he had done no
violence, neither was any deceit found in his mouth. Yet
it pleased the Lord to bruise him...he was numbered with
the transgressors; and he bare the sin of many, and made
intercession for the transgressors.* (Isaiah 53:3-12)

I am almost sure the religious leaders overlooked this passage in
Isaiah, because how could this be the Messiah? After all, did not Isaiah
also prophesy about One who will sit on the throne of David to order
it and establish it with judgment and justice. Surely this couldn't be
that man! What was Jesus doing? What was His purpose in coming as
a baby born in a manger? It is interesting to note that Isaiah said, *"Of
the increase of his government, there shall be no end..."* A government is
another form of a kingdom. In fact, it is an ever increasing kingdom,
to which there shall be no end. Many believers have adopted the belief
that this earth and everything in it is going to be destroyed. Is this
what the Bible teaches? Will there be an end to this world in which we
live in? A majority of people that go to church believe this is so. My
only question is: why would God create such a magnificent world for
us to live in only to destroy it? Maybe we should ponder this question
for a while.

When Jesus came into the world as a baby, He was raised by His
mother, a Jewish girl, along with His earthly father, Joseph. Having
lived His life as a young boy, He later found Himself speaking with
many teachers of the law and asking questions, eventually showing
Himself to the world and walked in Kingdom authority. Jesus came
with the Kingdom and of that same Kingdom, there shall be no end. I
love what Daniel said:

> *And in the days of these kings shall the God of heaven set up a kingdom, which shall never be destroyed: and the kingdom shall not be left to other people, but it shall break in pieces and consume all other kingdoms, and it shall stand forever.* (Daniel 2:44)

Jesus came to establish a Kingdom. John did not come preaching a religion, but a Kingdom. That Kingdom came with signs and wonders. It is crucial for us to understand the secrets and mysteries of the Kingdom. Listen to what Jonathan Welton said,

> *The Kingdom came in the manger, and was proclaimed by John the Baptist, explained and demonstrated by Jesus, confirmed in the covenant of forgiveness at the last supper...and passed to the Apostolic ambassadors before His ascension. Then it grew through the book of Acts to reach the inhabited and civilized world...At this point, the Kingdom is here and now; it has been here for two-thousand years, and it is growing and will continue to grow.*

It is not my intent to confuse or cause debate within the church, yet when we hear the term kingdom, we so often associate it with the end of this world and all life as we know it. Can we merge the doctrine of the kingdom and eschatology into the same arena? Many churches and ministries have taught and believed that the Kingdom of God is not necessary or relevant for our time, but rather will only exist and manifest in the future. How they interpret it, is they see God holding back certain things from the church, and is reserving them for the future when He sets up His final Kingdom here on earth.

What many Christian believers should realize is this: the Kingdom is here, but not yet. It has been given in a measure, but not in its fulness. We are living in exciting times. So very often we tend to look vertically, rather than horizontally. Again, this is not a teaching on eschatology, rapture, or end times.

The Kingdom in Our Midst

On the contrary, we are in the Kingdom now and it is growing and expanding. We still have more ground to take. In Luke 17:20-21, Jesus said,

> *Once, having been asked by the Pharisees when the kingdom of God would come, Jesus replied, "The Kingdom of God does not come with your careful observation, nor will people say, 'Here it is' or 'There it is' because the kingdom of God is within you.* (Luke 17:20-21)

The *New American Standard Version* says, *"...is in your midst."* What we must first understand is that this is very foundational for believers today. There are possibly millions of Christians in the world today that are wondering the same thing and asking, *"When will the kingdom of God come?"*

Jesus said it cannot be observed, nor be directed towards a particular location. What did He mean by this? The Jews, at that time, had the understanding that merely following the law would instill that same law into the hearts and mind of the people of the Kingdom. Regardless of your opinion of the Kingdom, it is not going to come through careful study and observation.

How is the Kingdom of God going to come? When is the Kingdom of God coming? Jesus said it very simply, *"The Kingdom of God is in your midst!"* In other words, He said, *"It's Me! I'm here! My name is Jesus Christ!"* Jesus was in their midst. He was and is the embodiment of Yahweh, the incarnation of God. He was the manifestation of the Kingdom in the flesh and demonstrated it in everything He said and did. He was put on display to show what everything should look like in the Kingdom of God. He was a living example of what a life fully surrendered and submitted to God should look like.

I would submit to you that you can be a living representative on earth, here and now, and become a reflection of the glory and the nature of the risen King. This is our duty and responsibility as Kingdom citizens. It is not merely to fill an empty pew or chair every Sunday morning, but rather to allow the glorified King of kings to manifest Himself in and through you in this lifetime. Stop waiting for things to happen and start making them happen. Become an agent of change and watch the Kingdom of God impact this generation!

CHAPTER 3

Kingdom Responsibilities & Mandate

When we hear the word responsibility, we often cringe because it is associated with other words like obligation or duty. It is referenced to the idea of corporate responsibility. What does this mean? Any leader, whether in a church, business, or country, has a moral or corporate responsibility towards the people that they are caring for. A simpler example would be parents caring for their biological or adopted children. This usually involves discipline, providing for their education, medical treatment, and well-being. It is, therefore, a sad situation that many Christians don't have a sense of responsibility for anything or anyone when it comes to the Kingdom of God. We have to consider certain facts and look intently at the Body of Christ. We have to wonder what is happening? Have we neglected our God-given responsibility and mandate as Kingdom citizens?

In every kingdom, certain obligations and responsibilities are carried out, just like any other country in the world today. What are those responsibilities and obligations? Throughout history, there have been diverse groups taking up the cause of dictatorships, such as Communism and Nazism. From the beginning of time, man has had within himself a natural state of mind called dominance. Throughout Scripture, we are bombarded with analogies and depictions of a kingdom. One of the greatest examples is found in the book of Genesis when the world and everything in it was created. In Genesis 1:26, we read,

> *And God said, Let us make man in our image, after our likeness, and let them have dominion over the fish of the sea, and over the fowl of the air, and over the cattle, and over all the earth, and over every creeping thing that creepeth upon the earth.* (Genesis 1:26)

The *King James Version* uses the word, *dominion*. What is this? According to *Webster's Dictionary*, it is defined as: *"the land that a ruler or government controls."* We also find another definition is the root word, *domain*. It's also defined as: *"a territory over which dominion is exercised."* This is where the word *kingdom* is derived from. It is a king's domain! It is the territory over which the king has rulership and authority.

The passage referred to earlier says, *"Let them have dominion..."* In other words, God, during the time of creation, was trying to establish a territory here on planet earth. But who was going to have dominance over that territory? Many people may not agree with this, but WE are given dominion over all the earth. Yes, God is King, and this world belongs to Him, but He still needs someone or some people to lord over this kingdom we call Earth. Listen to what the Psalmist said, *"The heaven, even the heavens, are the Lord's: but the earth has He given to the children of men"* (Psalm 115:16). Since the beginning of time, God has wanted to establish a Kingdom, a domain, but He needed and wanted someone to rule over and care for it. I am also thinking of the word, stewardship. This is in fact tied to the word responsibility. We would be surprised of how much the Bible speaks of stewardship. What is stewardship? It is the act of responsible planning and the management of resources. This usually has its involvement in the area of the environment, nature, economics, health, property, information, and theology.

Who is in Authority?

There was an event that happened during the time of Creation. Many of us are familiar with the fall of man. In the book of Genesis, Satan came in the form of a snake and tempted Adam and Eve, thus nullifying their God-given responsibilities as Kingdom representatives. We read that their eyes were opened and they saw their nakedness and immediately clothed themselves. The Bible tells us they were driven from the Garden of Eden. The God-given authority and dominion was stripped from them. Remember, when we read in the book of Genesis, *"And God said, Let us make man in our image, after our likeness, and let them have dominion..."* (Genesis 1:26). What happened to that authority? Who was it given to? We find an interesting statement in the Gospel of Luke,

> *The devil led him (Jesus) up to a high place and showed him in an instant all the kingdoms of the world. And he said unto him, I will give you all their authority and splendour, for it has been given to me, and I can give it to anyone I want.* (Luke 4:5,6 Emphasis added)

This would almost cause us to think and believe that Satan had control over the whole earth since the time Adam and Eve fell. However, we must consider some facts for a moment. Yes, Satan was an active participant in the world since the dawn of creation and has been reaping destruction upon the hearts and minds of humanity since. J.D. King said, *"Satan has never had full legal jurisdiction in the earth. Any 'lordship' he has possessed comes from robbery or deception."* He continues, *"He has no right to anything in God's creation. Although having no right to exert his will, he nevertheless found a way to grab hold of man's delegated authority. He wrestled a piece of humanity's power in the fall and is now using that to subjugate the land."* After being crucified and then resurrected, Jesus came to His disciples,

> *All power (authority and dominion) has been given to Me in heaven and in earth. Go ye therefore, and teach all nations, baptizing them in the name of the Father, and of the Son,*

and of the Holy Ghost: Teaching them to observe all things whatsoever I have commanded you: and, lo, I am with you alway, even unto the end of the world. (Matthew 28:18-20)

Many denominations and Bible translators have called this the *Great Commission*, but it holds another critical truth within it besides going into all the world and preaching the gospel. It is what we have been taught for decades. More and more ministers are traveling overseas to different nations of the world proclaiming the good news of Jesus Christ. Churches send missionaries and financial support to many poverty stricken nations throughout the year. There is nothing wrong with that, but unless we understand our role and responsibility as Kingdom people, we miss a very fundamental principle of our mission on earth. Jesus said, *"All power..."* We can assume that through His death, burial, and resurrection, He had stripped Satan of this power and gave it back to man. Since the day he fell from heaven, Satan had wanted that authority. He went so far to think that he could sit higher than God Himself. Of course, many Christians know that Satan is a deceiver and a liar and therefore, cannot be trusted.

The disciples then later came to Jesus at His ascension and asked, *"Lord, are you at this time going to restore the kingdom to Israel"* (Acts 1:6)? Jesus responded quickly, *"It is not for you to know the times or dates the Father has set by his own authority. But you..."* (Acts 1:7,8). I can almost hear Jesus say, *"I am not going to do it, you are! You are the ones to whom I give back authority and dominion, and the Holy Spirit will come upon you to empower you in all your doings for the Kingdom of God!"* What a wonderful, yet challenging responsibility we have as children of God.

What Do We Do?

In every kingdom, there are princes, subjects, lords, citizens, and ambassadors. Pay close attention for a moment to that one word, *ambassador.* What is an ambassador? What is the role of an ambassador? We can quickly identify an ambassador as a representative. An ambassador is a political appointee whose job is to represent and speak for his or her home government before the rulers of other countries. They represent their country while working and living in the country to which they've been appointed. Paul used the word, *ambassador* to identify the role of the believer in Jesus in 2 Corinthians 5:20, *"Now then we are ambassadors for Christ, as though God did beseech you by us: we pray you in Christ's stead, be reconciled to God."* As ambassadors, we are to be representatives of Christ here on Earth. In the following verses, Jesus exemplifies some statements and responsibilities of an ambassador:

> *Then answered Jesus and said unto them, 'Verily, verily I say unto you, The Son can do nothing of Himself, but what He seeth the Father do: for what things soever He doeth, these also the Son likewise.* (John 5:19)

Another interesting point regarding the position and responsibility of an ambassador is he is not his own. What do I mean by this? First, he must have knowledge of the kingdom and the king. Secondly, he must have the wisdom of the king so that his message and purpose will be persuasive. Thirdly, an ambassador's message and purpose is portrayed through his character. He not to remain neutral in these responsibilities, but rather grow and continue to grow. How is an ambassador not his own? When a man or woman is appointed as an ambassador to any country or nation, his home country has a responsibility to care for that ambassador. The country, from which he came, has the moral obligation to take on his needs of his family, finances, and property. It is why Jesus said, *"Therefore I tell you, do not worry about your life, what you will eat, or about your body, what you will wear...after all such things, and your Father knows that you need them"* (Luke 12:22,30). As citizens of the kingdom, we are, by rights, granted the resources of the Kingdom of God.

Ye Must Be Born Again

One of the associate pastors in the church my family and I attend preached a beautiful message that I will never forget. The text was from a familiar portion of Scripture,

> *There was a man of the Pharisees, named Nicodemus, a*
> *ruler of the synagogue. The same came to Jesus by night, and*
> *said unto him, Rabbi, we know that thou art a man come*
> *from God: for no man can do these miracles that thou doest,*
> *except God be with him. Jesus answered and said unto him,*
> *Verily, verily I say unto thee, Except a man be born again,*
> *he cannot see the kingdom of God.* (John 3:1-3)

We have all read this passage and maybe even preached from it. Throughout the centuries, there has been a strong emphasis on the doctrine of being *born again*. Whole ministries and denominations have made it a priority to get people *born again*. Bertram L. Gaines said,

> *Let's consider the new birth for a moment. Here is a*
> *message that Jesus preached only one time, to one guy, in*
> *the middle of the night (no crowds were present)! If you*
> *were to gauge Jesus' theology by today's evangelical sermons,*
> *you would think that the new birth was the only message*
> *he ever preached.*

Most Christians today become very contentious when someone speaks against the doctrine of the new birth experience. There is nothing wrong with it. It is crucial, but we must take to heart what Jesus was saying in this passage.

The first thing we must realize is Jesus was speaking of the Kingdom of God and He was also speaking to a man who knows this Hebrew God. This man, Nicodemus, was an educated man who knew the Scriptures, the Torah. In fact, he had studied under the religious system since childhood, and had become, as the Bible says, a ruler of the Jews and a man of the Pharisees. Jesus then responded to him and said, *"... he cannot see the Kingdom of God."* Right away our minds automatically think of entering the gates of heaven when we die or when Jesus comes back again. But we must remember, Jesus hasn't changed the subject, He is still speaking in context to what Nicodemus was asking Him about. Nicodemus said, *"for no man can do these miracles...except God be with him"* (John 3:2). It might sound like Jesus changed the subject. Nicodemus was only asking, *"How are you doing these miracles?"* Jesus answered, *"A man must be born again..."* Does this mean that Nicodemus would have to say the sinners prayer, give his heart and life to Jesus, and have his name written down in the Lamb's Book of Life? What is really being taught here in this passage about being born again? I remember a few years ago, I watched an old movie about boxing. The boxer was warming up to enter the ring, when he made this statement to his friends, *"Man, I feel born again!"* What was he talking about? Was he referring to the Christian experience of being born again? No! He was speaking about coming alive and feeling like a brand new man. As Jesus answered Nicodemus' question, He was not talking about becoming a brand new Christian, as most Christians believe, because Nicodemus was already a believer. Jesus was, however, speaking about the reviving of one's spirit and experiencing something greater from the Lord. Those disciples that were in the Upper Room on the day of Pentecost began as your average, ordinary, every day, law-observing Jews, but when the Holy Spirit came upon them, they became born again! Jesus said, if you want to see these miracles, you must become born again! Remember Jesus also spoke of, *"...you cannot see the kingdom of God."* Jesus was saying, *"Hey Nicodemus, if you want to operate in Kingdom power and authority, then you must become born again, be made alive, be revived, be rejuvenated, and be endued with power from on high!"* This man, Nicodemus, needed to come into Kingdom power and authority and realize His mandate and responsibility. As Kingdom representatives and ambassadors, it is also our mandate and responsibility to exercise that power and authority here on Earth.

No Greater Faith

Another interesting truth we find in the life of Jesus was when a Roman centurion came looking for Him to come and heal his servant, who was sick and dying. The story starts out this way:

> *And when Jesus was entered into Capernaum, there
> came unto him a centurion, beseeching him, And saying,
> Lord, my servant lieth at home sick of the palsy, grievously
> tormented. And Jesus saith unto him, I will come and heal
> him. The centurion answered and said, Lord, I am not
> worthy that thou shouldest come under my roof: but speak
> the word only, and my servant shall be healed. For I am a
> man under authority, having soldiers under me: and I say
> to this man, Go, and he goeth; and to another, Come, and
> he cometh; and to my servant, Do this, and he doeth it.
> When Jesus heard it, he marveled, and said unto them that
> followed, Verily I say unto, I have not found so great faith,
> no, not in Israel.* (Matthew 8:5-10 Emphasis added)

This portion of Scripture has been used to describe and demonstrate the kind of faith we are supposed to operate in. If we are not careful, we risk missing an important message in these passages. Jesus was ready and willing to go with this centurion to heal his servant, but then he stopped Jesus and said, *"No, I am not worthy to have you come under my roof, but speak the word only, and my servant shall be made whole! For I am a man under authority."* In other words, he was pointing out his position of authority to Jesus. Why? He demonstrated to Jesus that he knew the inner operations of kingdom authority. Craig Keener said, *"The centurion's response demonstrates that he (backed by Rome's authority) understands the principle of authority that Jesus exercises. Roman soldiers were very disciplined and followed orders very carefully; they provided the ultimate model of discipline and obedience to the Roman Empire."* Somehow, this Roman centurion recognized that Jesus was a King and understood kingdom concepts. He was very familiar with the line of authority through the Roman Empire. He said, *"I tell this one, 'Go' and he goes; and that one, 'Come' and he comes. I say to my servant, 'Do this' and he does it."* He also said, *"For I myself am a man under authority, with soldiers under me."* When he would command those soldiers under him, his power and authority were not only his own, but filtered through the line of authority from headquarters, which was Rome. The words, orders, and commands to his soldiers were just as valid and effective as though they were hearing from the Emperor himself. This is why the centurion said to Jesus, *"just speak the word only,"* because he understood the line of authority. Jesus was amazed at this kind of thinking! He stated clearly to His disciples, *"I tell you the truth, the Son can do nothing by himself..."* (John 5:19). Jesus was using the line of authority given to Him by His Father, who was in Heaven (headquarters), and just by speaking a word only, anything was possible at any time and any place. Yes, this story is about great faith and Jesus simply speaking a word, but it involves so much than what we have heard. This story portrays a strong emphasis on kingdom authority and power. Jesus said to the centurion, *"Go! It will be done just as you have believed it would. His servant was healed that very hour"* (Matthew 8:13)!

You Have a Purpose and a Destiny

God created us with a purpose. He created you and me with a purpose. There are seven billion people in the world today, and not one of them was born by accident. Although many people believe they were an accident and have heard the words, either from an abusive parent, relative or friend, that they were a biological accident. Your birth mother may have had a one-night stand with some stranger and you may never know who the father is. But you must understand, when God creates something, He doesn't create it as an experiment; He creates and designs with a purpose in mind! Everyone of us has a time to be born and a time to die and it doesn't matter if we were born out of wedlock or in wedlock. You were born because God has a specific plan and purpose for your life. One of the greatest statements I've ever heard was, *"When God creates something, He creates it to succeed."* You, as a living person on this planet, have a plan and a purpose given by God. It's time you discover that plan and learn to walk and live in it.

CHAPTER 4

The Gospel of the Kingdom

Four hundred years had passed without any prophetic voice in the land, without one, *"Thus saith the Lord..."* And here comes a man with a prophetic voice, John the Baptist echoed those words, *"Every valley shall be filled, and every mountain and hill shall be brought low; and the crooked shall be made straight, and the rough ways shall be made smooth"* (Luke 3:5). His message attacked the spiritual lethargy of his day and confronted the cause of sin. His spirit was distraught because the commands of God were broken, the Sabbath day rest was dishonored, and the Father's house was made desolate. What did John have? He did not have the backing of several hundred people pledging to pay his salary. He did not have a microphone in one hand and a Bible in the other. He did not have three or four cameras following his every movement while he preached. He did not have a fancy private jet to transport him back and forth from the Jordan River to the nearest five-star hotel. His company was, nothing more than the wild beasts while he had made his bed on the shorelines of the River Jordan. It was there in the wilderness that he spoke a language no one has ever heard before, but they knew he was speaking the truth in a wicked and perverse generation. He said, *"And now the ax is laid unto the root of the trees: every tree therefore which bringeth not forth not good fruit is hewn down and cast into the fire"* (Luke 3:9). The one thing John the Baptist carried was the anointing of the Holy Spirit. John was soon to face death at the hands of Herod. He knew very well that God anointed and appointed prophets had very short life expectancies. Jesus, being grieved at the imprisonment of John the Baptist, took upon Himself the mantle of anointing and ministry and ventured out. In Mark 1:14-15 it reads,

> *Now after John was put in prison, Jesus came into Galilee,*
> *preaching the gospel of the kingdom of God. And saying,*
> *The time is fulfilled, and the kingdom of God is at hand;*
> *repent ye, and believe the gospel.* (Mark 1:14,15)

Jesus took on the similar message as John the Baptist and boldly proclaimed, *"Blessed are the poor in the spirit, for theirs is the Kingdom of heaven"* (Matthew 5:3). Jesus was troubled at the lack of spiritual things that made the people spiritually weak. He was amazed at their lack of understanding about the God they claimed to know. He was not necessarily concerned so much with their natural state of being poor, but more with the spiritual barrenness that kept them from entering into the Kingdom. He came not to create something new, but rather, to restore something that had been lost and forgotten. He came preaching the good news of the gospel. That gospel was and is the gospel of the Kingdom of God. He did not come preaching salvation, healing, miracles, restoration, prosperity, deliverance, or hope. He came preaching a message that was the accumulation of all these things. Jesus knew that it would take a different message to gain the attention of the people. Throughout the centuries, we have heard countless sermons and messages about the Christian faith, but never has there been a message other than that of the Kingdom of God. Unfortunately, with the diverse opinions and numerous transitions in Christianity, the message of the gospel has suffered a significant spiritual fracture that continues today.

Gospel...Good News

What is the gospel of the Kingdom? First of all, the gospel is translated as, *good news.* I will speak more about this later. The message

John and Jesus came preaching wasn't just some gospel they fabricated. It was the gospel of the Kingdom of God. It was, in fact, the good news of the Kingdom. Paul preached this message in the last few verses of the book of Acts, *"Preaching the Kingdom of God, and teaching those things which concern the Lord Jesus Christ, with all confidence, no man forbidding him"* (Acts 28:31). This is Paul, who, under house arrest, or on parole for two whole years, received all those who came to him. He had this wonderful opportunity to impart something important into the lives of those who came to him.

Throughout the gospels, you will see the message of the Kingdom of God being taught by Jesus in the following Scriptures:

> *Jesus went about all Galilee, teaching in their synagogues, and preaching the gospel of the kingdom, and healing all manner of sickness and all manner of disease among the people.* (Matthew 4:23)

> *And Jesus went about all the cities and villages, teaching in their synagogues, and preaching the gospel of the kingdom, and healing every sickness and every disease among the people.* (Matthew 9:35)

> *But if I cast out devils by the Spirit of God, then the kingdom of God is come unto you.* (Matthew 12:28)

> *And he said unto them, I must preach the kingdom of God to other cities also..."* (Luke 4:43)

We can see that not only was the message of the Kingdom of God being proclaimed but it was also being demonstrated in the midst of the people. I remember hearing this statement some time ago, *"We don't need another definition of Christianity, but a demonstration of Christianity."* This does have some truth to it, but what if our definition of Christianity has been misinterpreted throughout the centuries? Yes, I believe we need to see more demonstration of the Kingdom, but when our definition of

Christianity and the Kingdom becomes right and accurate, we will see miracles and healings unlike we have ever seen before.

The Keys of the Kingdom

We find an interesting conversation between Jesus and Peter in Matthew 16,

> *When Jesus came to the region of Caesarea Philippi, he asked his disciples, "Who do people say the Son of Man is?" They replied, "Some say John the Baptist; others say Elijah; and still others, Jeremiah or one of the prophets." "But what about you?" he asked. "Who do you say I am?" Simon Peter answered, "You are the Messiah, the Son of the living God." Jesus replied, "Blessed are you, Simon son of Jonah, for this was not revealed to you by flesh and blood, but by my Father in heaven. And I tell you that you are Peter, and on this rock I will build my church, and the gates of Hades will not overcome it. I will give you the keys of the kingdom of heaven; whatever you bind on earth will be bound in heaven, and whatever you loose on earth will be loosed in heaven.* (Matthew 16:13-19)

Most of us are familiar with this story. Jesus asked Peter, *"Who do you say that I am?"* Peter had received a supernatural word from heaven when he replied, *"You are the Christ, the Son of the Living God!"* Jesus' reply was, *"for this was not revealed to you by flesh and blood, but by my Father in heaven!"* Why is this so important? The Kingdom of God cannot be understood or explained by mere intellectualism or knowledge, but by the Spirit of God only. Jesus was saying in this passage, *"Because you did not receive this by flesh and blood, but by the Spirit, I am going to give you the keys to the Kingdom!"* Keys represent responsibility. If I give you the keys to my vehicle, you are responsible for it. You are responsible for its safety, for purchasing gasoline, making sure it is kept clean inside and out, and for it not being stolen. We have been given the keys, or the responsibilities of the Kingdom. God has entrusted us, as His sons and daughters, with the keys of the Kingdom. Not to hold them to ourselves, but to understand and learn them by His Holy Spirit, and unlock the doors to blessings and power for us and those around us.

We see an example of the life of Nicodemus. When Nicodemus asked Jesus about the Kingdom of God, and how He was doing all those miracles, Jesus was amazed. Even though Nicodemus was considered a teacher of the law, a Pharisee, he could not understand the Kingdom. Even after reading and studying the accounts of Moses, Abraham, and other supernatural events portrayed in the Torah, he himself was lacking spiritual power and authority. After all, he was supposed to be demonstrating this power. Nicodemus said, *"How can this be?"* Jesus said to him, *"You are Israel's teacher...and do you not understand these things?...I have spoken to you of earthly things, and you do not believe; how then will you believe if I speak of heavenly things"* (John 3:9-12)? I can just imagine Nicodemus entering into the synagogue as a young, eager student. But after years of study and learning, perhaps he may have lost that spiritual passion and fervency he once carried. Paul said to the church in Corinth, *"We know that "We all possess knowledge." But knowledge puffs up..."* (1 Corinthians 8:1). Perhaps Nicodemus lost it as a result of his passion to learn and study. I am not implying that studying and learning is an erroneous idea, but perhaps it came at a great cost.

It is my hope and desire that the church today would walk in the full capacity of that same power and authority of the Kingdom. Is the world ready for such a display of power, or should I ask: is the church ready for such a display of Kingdom authority and power? Jesus said, *"And this gospel of the kingdom shall be preached in all the world for a witness unto all nations, and then the end shall come"* (Matthew 24:14). This is the gospel of the Kingdom of God.

Something New?

They went to Capernaum, and when the Sabbath came, Jesus went into the synagogue and began to teach. The

> *people were amazed at his teaching, because he taught them as one who had authority, not as the teachers of the law. Just then a man in their synagogue who was possessed by an impure spirit cried out, "What do you want with us, Jesus of Nazareth? Have you come to destroy us? I know who you are—the Holy One of God!" "Be quiet!" said Jesus sternly. "Come out of him!" The impure spirit shook the man violently and came out of him with a shriek. The people were all so amazed that they asked each other, "What is this? A new teaching—and with authority! He even gives orders to impure spirits and they obey him." News about him spread quickly over the whole region of Galilee.* (Mark 1:21-28)

Jesus had just cast the devil out of one man in the synagogue. The gospel of Mark, chapter 1 reads, *"The people were all so amazed that they asked each other, "What is this? A new teaching..."* (Mark 1:27). In the same chapter, we see Jesus coming into Galilee preaching the gospel of the Kingdom of God. It was being demonstrated through the casting out of devils. As soon as Jesus embarked on His journey as the One who was to come, He explained and walked in Kingdom authority. This was the gospel in manifestation. This was the Kingdom.

It is amusing that when I begin to talk about the Kingdom of God to people, not just any people, but Christian people, they are amazed and shocked at some of the things I share concerning the Kingdom of God. Most of these same people have been saved and going to church for several years. Bertram L. Gaines continues, *"...it's probably one of the most neglected topics in theology. In fact, for all of the Lord's emphasis on it, it is not even designated as a branch of theology. We have hamartiology (the doctrine of sin), soteriology (the doctrine of redemption), ecclesiology (the doctrine of the church), eschatology (the doctrine of the end-times), and several other 'ologies, but no Kingdomology."* The doctrine of the Kingdom of God was not something new when Jesus came to preach and declare it to His generation, rather, it was a doctrine that had been lost and forgotten through the centuries. It was something He needed to reintroduce and demonstrate.

The Gospel

We have heard this term for centuries. The word was derived from an old English word and has its origin in the meaning of, *"good news,"* or *"glad tidings."* We see these words being used by the angel, Gabriel, when he appeared to those lonesome shepherds in the field in Luke, *"And, lo, the angel of the Lord came upon them, and the glory of the Lord shone round about them: and they were sore afraid. And the angel said unto them, Fear not: for, behold, I bring you good tidings of great joy, which shall be to all people"* (Luke 2:9,10). We see that the good tidings was good news, and it shall be to all people. Notice that the angel did not isolate it just to a particular group such as the Jews, but said it was for all people. The angel knew that the message of the Messiah and His Kingdom would be to all people in every generation.

The Apostle Paul made this declaration to the church in Corinth,

> *Now, brothers and sisters, I want to remind you of the gospel I preached to you, which you received and on which you have taken your stand. By this gospel, you are saved, if you hold firmly to the word I preached to you. Otherwise, you have believed in vain. For what I received I passed on to you as of first importance: that Christ died for our sins according to the Scriptures.* (1 Corinthians 15:1-3)

According to most church doctrines and beliefs, when we define or speak of, *"the gospel"* we often refer to the life of Christ, primarily His death, resurrection, ascension, and His return. There are different variations to consider. There may be those who would answer, the gospel is Matthew, Mark, Luke, and John. What was THE Gospel? Along with the Scripture references we have already used, the Bible states, *"Now after John was put in prison, Jesus came into Galilee, preaching the gospel of the kingdom of God. And saying, The time is fulfilled, and the kingdom of God is at hand; repent ye, and believe the gospel"* (Mark 1:14,15). The gospel is not a gospel at all without the Kingdom of God. In fact, it should be translated as, *"the good news of the gospel of the Kingdom of God."* This is what the world is waiting to hear. The world today is filled with negativity, from the news, social media, the political arena, university campuses, and so on. What we need in the world today is some good news!

There have been countless campaigns, events, crusades, meetings, and so on, all in the name of evangelism, or as modern day churches would call it, *"getting souls saved."* This has been the form of gospel presentation throughout the last few decades. There is nothing wrong with these attempts and I appreciate their hearts and the motivation behind it, but what are we missing? What has been the lost ingredient to preaching the gospel? Over the centuries, it has been the gospel of healing, salvation, deliverance, miracles, church growth, children's ministry, worship, and while all of these are good, there still seems to be a very large portion missing in regards to our attempt to win people to the Kingdom. There is a fascinating story that Pastor Steve Gray shares in his book, *My Absurd Religion,* in which he receives a visit from a door-to-door preacher. The conversation went like this:

(Knock on door)
Me: Yeah?
Stranger: Are you saved?
Me: Huh?
Stranger: If you don't know, then you probably aren't.
Me: Know what?
Stranger: If you were to die today, do you know if you would go to heaven?
Me: Go to heaven?
Stranger: Yeah, if you died today would you go to heaven?
Me: I don't know.
Stranger: Would like to know how to get to heaven?
Me: If I died?
Stranger: Yeah, if you died today.
Me: Can I ask you a question?

Stranger: Sure.

Me: Do you have anything for me if I don't die?

Stranger: What do you mean?

Me: I don't think I am going to die today. So what have you got for me if I live? What will God do for me, right here, right now?

Stranger: I don't know.

Me: Come back when you find out.

The majority of gospel influence and emphasis has been on the idea of your destination when you die. The message today is, *"If you were to die today, where would you go?"* Of course, many of us understand there are only two destinations, Heaven, and Hell. Was this the same gospel message that was preached by Peter, Paul, and the other disciples of Jesus? Was it preached at all in the book of Acts, or by others throughout history? Christianity and the Kingdom of God, as preached today, have primarily been about a destination, rather than a journey. My wife, in her personal testimony, grew up hearing the message of the rapture and hell. In fact, this was one of the main reasons why she came to Jesus and invited Him into her heart. But since that time, she lived the rest of her Christian life in fear. Why? She feared that she would one day miss the rapture or go to hell if she ever backslid or turned away from God. I thank God she no longer lives in this attitude of fear. Jonathan Welton shares some interesting insight in regards to this. He said, *"Some say that having a fearful future motivates evangelism."* He continues, *"Many have been brought into Christianity through fear of hell, judgment, or rapture; they then have had to spend years untangling their spiritual walk from the fear into which they were birthed."* Unfortunately, this is has been the mentality of so many Christians today. We must remember and take to heart that Jesus came with good news. This is what the gospel of the Kingdom of God is all about!

What Do We Preach?

Dr. Derek Morphew writes,

> *The theme of the Kingdom as preached by Jesus Christ unites the whole flow of biblical truth, from Moses, through the Prophets, the Writings, the Gospels, the Epistles, and the Revelation of John.*

We have to realize this one essential truth; the gospel of the Kingdom of God is the central culmination of the entire Bible. Yes, we must preach repentance, the baptism in the Holy Spirit, healing, faith, grace, and a host of others to the world and the church, but let us never forget that all these doctrines and teachings all point to the one centralized message: that is the Kingdom of God.

This gospel message is about the Kingdom of our God. The Kingdom of God is here, but not yet. One of my mentors and Bible teacher said it this way, *"It is here in a measure, but not in its fullness."* It is our duty and responsibility as believers in Jesus to bring the Kingdom to Earth. If I may pose a question: are there any sicknesses in heaven? Are there any diseases in heaven? Are there any bad attitudes in heaven? Is there any darkness, fear, or anxiety in heaven? None of these exist in heaven. Jesus wanted to us to pray for the reality of heaven to be present here on earth. Pastors and churches want to see change, healing and miracles, salvation, and deliverance in their churches and ministries but generally don't see the things which they desire to see. This is why we must pray, *"Your Kingdom come, Your will be done, on earth as it is in heaven!"* This is an amazing prayer! Jesus is basically saying, pray that the reality of God's Kingdom, God's heavenly glory be manifested here on earth. This is the secret to walking in supernatural power and seeing the miraculous hand of God at work in our midst. We must pray this everywhere we go and in everything we do. This is and must be the gospel message. Anything that doesn't appear like the reality of heaven, we have the right as children of God to come against it. This is how we pray and this is how we change the world!

CHAPTER 5

Kingdom Advancement

How do we associate the idea and doctrine of the Kingdom with advancement and expansion? Never has any kingdom or nation in history expanded or advanced without the act of war. It is unfortunate that it involves armed conflict between two or more nations and societies, and eventually births collective aggression, destruction, and usually, a high casualty rate. Every so often, there can also be civilian or non-combatant casualties. How do we relate this to the Kingdom of God?

Our history is filled with acts of violence and war, not against any other forces of nature, but man against his fellow man. Time will not permit me to speak of the wars in biblical times, from Abraham to Moses, Joshua to Gideon, and David to Nehemiah. In every war, strategic planning and preparation are involved. Throughout history, there have been extraordinary advancements in weaponry and developments on a large scale. Fashioning and forging were, however, very complex and time-consuming. The use of stone tools eventually gave way to the manufacturing of bronze weapons and armour. This was a significant shift in the history of war. Inventions such as the axe, armour, the helmet, the bow and arrow, later gave birth to numerous tactical innovations. There was also a significant increase in mobility, like the invention of the wheel and chariots. It was inventions such as these that assisted great victories in ancient warfare.

Leaders in War

History has recorded countless events of different nations and individual leaders who conquered and expanded their empires through means of war. Most of us would be familiar with a man named Alexander the Great, who served as King of Macedonia from 336-323 BC. It is said that during his time of leadership, he united Greece, reestablished the Corinthian League, and conquered the Persian Empire. He later became king upon his father's death in 336 BC and went on to conquer most of the known world of his day. He is called, *"The Great"* both for his military genius and his diplomatic skills in handling the various populaces of the regions he conquered.

We also have a Mongolian warrior named Genghis Khan, who created the largest empire in the world. At the establishment of his empire, he conquered and destroyed individual tribes in many parts of Northeast Asia. It is said that Genghis Khan possessed outstanding military tactics and merciless brutality, which gave him control over most of Central and Eastern Mongolia. He understood many of the tactics and their motivations of his enemies. He also utilized the spy network and was quick to adapt to their new found technologies. They developed and equipped themselves with a sophisticated signalling system of smoke and burning torches. Along with these, large drums sounded commands to charge, and further orders were conveyed with flag signals. Through such inventions and technologies, Genghis Khan was assured victory every time.

Another such man was Napoleon Bonaparte, who was a French military leader and emperor who conquered much of Europe in the early nineteenth century. He quickly rose through the ranks of the army during the French Revolution of 1789-1799. After seizing political power in France in 1799, he crowned himself Emperor in 1804. Shrewd, ambitious, and a skilled military strategist, Napoleon successfully waged war against various coalitions of European nations and expanded his empire.

Adolph Hitler has made his mark in the annals of warfare history, some of which we wish had never taken place, but despite all he did, he still played a role in history as the leader of the German Nazis. It was a dark time in human history, which held an unfathomable scale of destruction. They launched a racist war of annihilation and, in the process, spawned the cancer, which we now know as, the Holocaust. The events that transpired in the Holocaust can only be described as humanity at its worst. It is said that nearly two-thirds of the Jewish population was annihilated. Hitler and his armies had a goal in mind which was the eradication of the entire Jewish population. Many Jewish people were removed from their homes, banned from ordinary day-to-day society, and forced to live in the ghetto, and then starved to death. Many of the Jews died of exposure and disease. History records that the Nazis developed new ways to eliminate people, which included gas chambers which became the leading means of killing them. Some were experimented on, worked to death, and others were deliberately or systematically murdered. From 1933 to 1945, it was estimated that nearly 11 million Jews lost their lives at the hands of the Nazis. For the Jewish population, it was a nightmare they need not live out ever again.

Why am I sharing all of this? Every one of these leaders had one common goal in mind: world domination and control. This is not an uncommon natural state of the human mind. Since the beginning of time, man has had the natural God-given inclination and desire to rule. This is what the Bible describes as dominion. Unfortunately, in the world in which we live, wars have not decreased, but rather, have increased throughout the centuries. It has been said that many of world leaders possessed a vast number of weapons spurring mass destruction. Unfortunately, millions have lost their lives to these men. It is also interesting that many of these wars were triggered and initiated in the name of religion.

What Is Our War?

Yes, these were wars fought amongst human beings, with men killing one another. However, the Bible is very clear about the fact that in the Kingdom of God we fight a different enemy, *"...we wrestle not against flesh and blood, but against principalities, against powers, against the rulers of the darkness of this world, against spiritual wickedness in high places"* (Ephesians 6:12). We also find other verses to support this,

> *For though we walk in the flesh, we do not war according to the flesh.* (2 Corinthians 10:3)

> *For the weapons of our warfare not carnal (fleshly), but mighty through God to the pulling down of strongholds.* (2 Corinthians 10:4)

> *Dearly beloved, I beseech you as strangers and pilgrims, abstain from fleshly lusts, which war against the soul.* (1 Peter 2:11)

In Scripture, we also read of the different analogies used to describe weaponry and armour.

> *For the weapons of our warfare not carnal (fleshly), but mighty through God to the pulling down of strongholds.* (2 Corinthians 10:4 Emphasis added)

> *Put on the full armour of God, that ye may be able to stand against all the wiles (schemes) of the devil.* (Ephesians 6:11 Emphasis added)

> *The night is almost gone, and the day is near. Therefore, let us lay aside the deeds of darkness and put on the armour of light.* (Romans 13:12)

> *But since we are of the day, let us be sober, having put on the breastplate of faith and love, and as a helmet, the hope of salvation.* (1 Thessalonians 5:8)

One of my all time favourite verses in the Bible is Matthew 11:12, and this section is founded primarily on this verse,

> *From the days of John the Baptist until now the kingdom of heaven suffereth violence, and the violent take it by force.* (Matthew 11:12)

We have to remember that in every kingdom, there is going to be war. No kingdom in history has ever advanced and expanded without the act and violence of war. As Christians, we are at war! This life we call Christianity is a war, but we must also keep in mind what the writer said in Ecclesiastes, *"To everything there is a season, and a time to every purpose under the heaven...a time of war, and a time of peace"* (Ecclesiastes 3:1,8). There are also seasons of peace in the life of a believer when he can enjoy the life he has in Christ. But this does not exempt us from the seasons of war. Too many Christians get so caught up in the season of peace that they forget there is a war. Remember, wars are fought over power. There are two forces at work in our lives: the flesh and the spirit. Many of you have read the famous book called, *The Battlefield of the Mind* by Joyce Meyer, which goes into greater detail on the subject. There are also other forces at war on the battlefield of the mind. These are the forces of darkness, which are Satan and his demons fighting against the Spirit of God, Who is the Holy Spirit.

There is another war taking place: it is the advancement and expansion of the Kingdom of God. This is primarily about influence. We live in a world that is dominated by different influences. We have influences in our homes, in public schools, in colleges and universities, in various forms of government, among friends and family, and even from those to whom we are married. The only question is: who will win the war? On which side of the line will we find ourselves? We must remember that wars are fought and won through careful, strategic planning, and preparation.

Suffers Violence

What was Jesus referring to when He said, *"the kingdom of heaven suffers violence?"* There was a group of people during the time of Jesus called, *Zealots*. These people were initially a political group of people seeking to overthrow the Roman Empire through military force. They also sought after the idea of inciting a rebellion to force out the Romans from the Holy Land. Jesus used their zeal in a descriptive way for us to follow. The term violence is the definitive word to describe the application of force, or to use force, to inflict violence upon. The language Jesus used was a not a passive aggressive type, but an active force that we are to inflict upon the forces of evil. He also said, *"... and the violent take it by force!"* There is no passivity involved in the Kingdom of God. There is an all out war for the souls of humanity, for our families, our children, our spouses, our country, and the world. God is looking for such people to advance His Kingdom here on Earth.

Kingdom Expansion

When we speak of the idea of advancement, we are also speaking of expansion. The different historical figures discussed at the beginning of this section all had one common goal in mind and that was expansion. Expansion of what? Their kingdoms! God is also looking to expand His Kingdom. You are probably wondering, doesn't God own the whole world? Yes, He does, but we have to remember that He gives everyone on this entire world free-will and choice. We have a choice whether or not to serve and follow Him. Remember, earlier we spoke of influence. Where does the Kingdom of God have influence? Many years ago, it did have influence in our public schools and governmental systems. There was a powerful statement a few years ago, which played in huge role in my wanting to study more about the Kingdom of God. I heard a message a few years ago which said, *"Where you find the rule of God, there you will find the Kingdom of God."* You will not find the rule of God everywhere, and unfortunately, you will not find it in a lot of churches today. For many people around the world, you will find an acknowledgement of God somewhere, but you will not find His rule or influence. Remember, in every natural or physical kingdom, both past and present, they all desired to gain influence and control.

How is Kingdom expansion going to happen? When Jesus stepped on the scene and entered into full-time ministry, He used a lot of analogies and terms to help the people better understand His message, particularly things about the Kingdom of God. One term He used was the word, *apostle.* Most people in the church today are unfamiliar with the ministry of the Apostle. We have become more familiar and comfortable with the position of the pastor and maybe even the evangelist. What most don't realize is that the term, *apostle* was first introduced before the term pastor ever did. The word *pastor* came in around the time of the Protestant Reformation when they replaced the Old Testament office of the, *priest.* Pastors have only been used in the church for an estimated 500 years, but we are more accustomed and familiar with them than we are apostles. This, however, does not make the ministry of the pastor invalid in the church today. The ministry gift of the pastor is still very much needed and necessary in the Body of Christ. But we must never forget the structure and ministry gifts that God put in place. The ministry of the apostle is needed just as much as the ministry of the pastor. What most don't know and understand is that Jesus borrowed this term from the Roman world. It was a term used to describe *"one who is sent."* The church has somehow adopted the idea that Jesus just randomly came up with these terminologies. In actuality, most of the words He used were pretty common in the Roman world. The primary reason Jesus used the word, *"Apostle"* was because the Romans used the term to describe someone who was sent to perform a particular task. Mark W. Pfeifer said, *"In their world, an apostle was a person sent by the Emperor to expand the borders of the Roman Empire into uncharted territory. They would do so by leading a group of citizens to create a functioning colony that would establish a Roman foothold in uncharted territory where the kingdom could eventually expand."* We see this exemplified in the life of the disciples in Luke 6, where Jesus chose twelve of His apostles (sent ones) and sent them out. Mark Pfeifer continues, *"He chose the term that best described what His twelve disciples would have to do in order to achieve this mandate around the world."* In other words, it was a trial run for the disciples for kingdom expansion, because they were also commanded, not to go to the Gentiles, but unto the lost sheep of Israel (Matthew 10:5,6). Of course, we are familiar what happened after the ascension of Jesus. In Acts chapter 1 it says, *"And you shall be witnesses unto Me both in Jerusalem, and in all Judaea, and in Samaria, and unto the uttermost part of the earth"* (Acts 1:8) But before they could take on such a task they had to be empowered and filled with the Holy Spirit for kingdom expansion.

The Battle is not Yours Alone

We cannot fight this battle alone. We must have the Holy Spirit dwelling within us. Those disciples that gathered in the Upper Room knew they needed something and Someone to take up residency inside of them if they were to take the message of the Kingdom to the nations and advance that very Kingdom. One my favourite authors, Leonard Ravenhill, said, *"A man with an experience of God is never at the mercy of a man with an argument, for an experience of God that costs something is worth something, and does something."* We are going to come against our very own religious elite, just as Jesus faced His own in His time. We are going to encounter numerous intellectuals who will have the Bible supposedly figured out and explained from cover to cover.

There is an interesting observation that I want to make. It was not the Roman government that killed Jesus. It was religion that killed Him. How so? Jesus was faced with a religious system that was so far removed from spiritual matters that it got lost in tradition and political corruptness. So much so that when Jesus stepped on the scene of human affairs, He suffered more from those claiming God as their father than those outside the religious sphere. It became abundantly clear that when Jesus denounced the religious and said, *"...you who killed the prophets..."* (Luke 13:34), left a lasting impression on their minds up to the time they placed Him on that cross. Not to mention the "Woes!" he pronounced to them in Matthew 23. Still this war is taking place and, unfortunately, it is not with those outside the church, but those within the church walls. Over the course of church history, the church has suffered more from those within its four walls than from those outside. How sad! Don't you think its time we change that? It's up to you.

Revival Is War

When the church refers to the idea of revival and the presence of God invading, we often think of entertainment and a party. If we check church history, revival never came by way of entertainment and passivity; it came through warfare. Steve Gray said, *"Revival is not a party – it is a war. It comes as an invasion from heaven to shake the foundations of religion, to stir the waters of the soul and to restore honour to the name of the Lord. It is a war in which God sets some apart, sets some on fire and sets some aside."* He continues, *"War brings inner conflict. Whose side am I really on? What kind of lifestyle do I want for my family and me? Some want the God of the universe to host a revival party where everyone is singing and dancing; one wonders why the cries of war are not heard."* God is still looking for men and women who will be so filled with the unction and ability of the Spirit that nothing will detour and diminish them. I hope and pray we will be recognized when those demons cry out, *"Paul I know, and Jesus I know!"*

CHAPTER 6

The Citizen

We have talked a lot about the Kingdom and the King, who Jesus is, but what about the citizens of that Kingdom? Being a First Nation person living in Canada, I have citizenship with the country of Canada. I was born and raised here in Canada, which makes me a citizen. As a registered First Nation person living in Canada, I am recognized by the Federal Government and therefore, am entitled to a broad range of programs and services offered by both the Federal and Provincial Governments. I did not become a citizen of Canada because I was permitted to and was granted citizenship. I became a citizen because I was born here. I am honoured and consider it a privilege to be a First Nation person here in my home country of Canada. There is nowhere else in this physical world that I'd rather be than here.

What is a citizen? According to *Webster's Dictionary*, a citizen is *a native or naturalized member of a state or nation who owes allegiance to its government and is entitled to its protection.* In our nation of Canada, we have many people from other countries of the world coming and becoming citizens of our country. For whatever reason, many have fled their country of origin and entered into Canada and obtained their citizenship. Those from other countries wanting to become Canadian citizens, must realize there are rights and individual responsibilities to becoming a citizen of this great country.

Rights and Responsibilities

Our society is no stranger to these concepts. We have different ideas instituted in many corporations, businesses, and schools. For instance, in the construction industry, it says that we all have the right to a safe workplace and staying safe on the job is everyone's responsibility.

What is the difference between a right and responsibility? A right is *a freedom that is protected, such as the right to free speech and religion.* A responsibility is *a duty, or something you should do, the act of being responsible, or accountable, for something within one's power, control, or management.* These rights are what every human being deserves, no matter who they are or where they are from, so that we can all live in a world that is fair and just. It is something that affects both our lives and other people's lives.

Any and every kingdom must have citizens to function as such. Every kingdom, nation, or country survives off the backs of it citizens and vice-versa. A church organization would not be a church without members, and a business or corporation cannot operate or function without employees.

As citizens of the Kingdom of God, we are privileged to all the guarantees of the King. We have been born into this Kingdom as sons and daughters. John writes, *"Yet to all who received Him, to those who believed in His name, He gave right to become children of God"* (John 1:12). In Colossians 1:13, its says, *"Who (the Father) hath delivered us from the power (dominion) of darkness, and hath translated (brought) us into the kingdom of his dear Son"* (Colossians 1:13 Emphasis added). Let us take a look at some of these rights and responsibilities as kingdom citizens.

Worship of the King

Our worship of the King is by far one of the most important aspects when discussing a king and his kingdom. We don't worship a king in our country, as in ancient times when citizens of the kingdom were expected to worship the king. We do not worship our Prime Minister, but we are to show honour towards him. The Apostle Peter said, *"Honour all men. Love the brotherhood. Fear God. Honour the king"* (1 Peter 2:17). Remember, Peter was speaking during a time of great persecution carried out through by the Roman Empire. Peter and others could have easily started a rebellion towards the Romans and the Emperor, yet he encouraged the believers to honour the Emperor, and even pray for him. This is strange to us, because in our Western culture, we know nothing of worshiping and bowing down towards a king. We are more likely to worship, revere, or follow certain sports athletes, Hollywood celebrities, famous rock or pop singers, or celebrated authors and speakers. We show all manner of appreciation towards men and women like this. We attend concerts, games, purchase books or magazines, hang posters or pictures, and spend hundreds of dollars, all in the name of the person or group we admire or cherish. There is an element of attraction to such people. We are drawn to these kinds of people because it is appealing to our minds, or our carnal nature, which is our flesh. The Bible warns us of such things. Paul gives the church in Rome an adamant admonition, *"And be not conformed to the pattern of this world, but be ye transformed by the renewing of your mind..."* (Romans 12:2). It is important that we remain in the Word of God on a regular basis and allow the Holy Spirit to conform us and teach us in the way we should go.

We have the example of the High Priest, who would go into the Holy of Holies, the most holy place, every year as a mediator for the people and offer a sin sacrifice on the day that we call the Day of Atonement. The book of Hebrews says, *"...the high priest alone once a year, not without blood, which he offered for himself, and for the errors (sins) of the people"* (Hebrews 9:7 Emphasis added). This duty was not to be taken lightly. The High Priest's life was on the line, and proper preparations were necessary. Can you imagine, for a moment, if we were ever given an opportunity to stand before Queen Elizabeth II? If we acknowledged her as, *"Hey Elizabeth! Great to see you!"* What do you think the consequence would be? We would more than likely experience some type of repercussions for our actions and be dismissed from her presence. Of course, there is a protocol. We would probably be instructed and advised to address her as, *"Your Majesty,"* or *"Your Highness,"* and so on.

I remember when I was working at a northern mine site. We were told that a certain dignitary could be visiting the mine. We were instructed, that in the event we crossed paths with him and his entourage, to address him as, *"Your Excellency."* The visitation was cancelled, so I never got the say it that day.

What is worship? It is an act of one's belief towards a deity. It may be performed individually, corporately, or brought about by a designated leader. We see many forms of worship throughout the Bible such as, lifted or raised hands, dancing, bowing down, shouting, etc. The Bible is filled with many illustrations concerning worship. As Canadians, we are privileged to live in a country where we have freedom of worship. How can we relate this to the Kingdom of God? First, we must understand that from a natural point of view, it is an expressed gratitude and appreciation to and of the king. It also involves a dependency on the king, which obligates the king to care for the citizens who proclaim him as king. When we worship the king, which in our case, as Christians, is worshiping King Jesus, He has obligations as our King to meet our needs and care for us. However, we have to check our motivation when it comes to praising the King, Jesus. Let's look at a few Scriptures concerning worship.

> *I am the Lord thy God, which have brought thee out of the land of Egypt, out of the house of bondage. Thou shalt have no other gods before me...for I the Lord thy God is a jealous God..."* (Exodus 20:2-6)

Give unto the Lord the glory due unto his name: bring an offering, and come before him: worship the Lord in the beauty of his holiness. (1 Chronicles 16:29)

But the hour cometh, and now is, when the true worshippers shall worship the Father in spirit and in truth: for the Father seeketh such to worship him. God is a Spirit: and they that worship him must worship him in spirit and in truth. (John 4:23-24)

Exalt ye the Lord our God, and worship at his footstool; for he is holy. (Psalm 99:5)

Therefore, I urge you, brothers, in view of God's mercy, to offer your bodies as living sacrifices, hold and pleasing to God – this is your spiritual act of worship. (Romans 12:1)

The four and twenty elders fall down before him that sat on the throne, and worship him and that liveth for ever and ever, and cast their crowns before the throne saying, Thou art worthy, O Lord, to receive glory and honour and power: for thou hast created all things, and for thy pleasure they are and were created. (Revelation 4:10,11)

Therefore, since we are receiving a kingdom that cannot be shaken, let us be thankful, and so worship God acceptably with reverence and awe. (Hebrews 12:28)

Thou, even thou, art Lord alone: thou hast made heaven, the heaven of heavens, with all their host, the earth, and all things that are therein, the seas, all that is therein, and thou preservest them all: and the host of heaven worshippeth thee. (Nehemiah 9:6)

> *All nations whom thou hast made shall come and worship*
> *before thee, O Lord; and shall glorify thy name.* (Psalm
> 86:9)

Through these Scriptures we have just read, we see we have the right and responsibility to enter into the holiest place and worship the King of kings. We must also consider it as a privilege. The Bible gives us the assurance that we can enter into that place with boldness and confidence. He is worthy of our worship!

Tithing & Giving

The second thing I want to look at is the concept of giving. In the church or religious world, we call this tithing. All kingdoms operate under a taxation system. It is a fee charged by a government (kingdom) on a product, income, or activity. The purpose of this tax system is to finance government expenditures, such as street lighting, maintenance, and city infrastructure. In ancient times, the citizens were allowed to participate in the process of maintaining the kingdom's infrastructure through taxation. This system also allowed the citizens to share in the kingdom's wealth and return a set portion of the king's resources back to the king. Jesus said this to His disciples, *"Give to Caesar what is Caesar's, and to God what is God's"* (Matthew 22:21). Everything in the Kingdom already belongs to the king; it is just simply passing through the hands of the citizens.

What are we talking about? Again, we are talking about the idea of tithing. As the Bible commands, we are to give a portion of our finances to our local church. The prophet Malachi said this, *"Bring ye all the tithe into the storehouse, that there may be meat in thine house, and prove me now herewith, said the Lord of hosts, if I will not open you the windows of heaven, and pour out a blessing, that there shall not be room enough to receive it"* (Malachi 3:10).

We are required, according to God's commands, to give ten percent of our gross income. It says in the book of Proverbs, *"Honour the Lord with your substance, and with the firstfruits of all thine increase"* (Proverbs

3:9). Where does the ten percent come from? In the book of Leviticus, it says, *"And all the tithe of the land, whether of the seed of the land or of the fruit of the tree, is the Lord's: it is holy unto the Lord"* (Leviticus 27:30). The book of Hebrews says, *"And Abraham gave him a tenth of everything"* (Hebrews 7:2, Genesis 14:20).

My wife and I make it a point in our lives that the portion of the tithe is taken out first and foremost. It is not a question in our household whether or not we are giving our tithe. I also want to point out that it is not a part of your bills. I don't even want to experience or know what will transpire if my wife and I ever fail to give our tithe to the house of God. It is unfortunate that there are many Christians and even churches that don't believe in the idea of tithing. They say it is an Old Testament practice and has no place in the New Testament. However, the Bible does speak about a tithe in the New Testament, Jesus mentioned it when He was talking to the religious leaders in Matthew 23:23. Giving is and should be a fundamental principle in the Kingdom of God for every believer in Christ. I am a firm believer in the area of giving of my tithe, and not only my tithe, but also an offering on top of that. There is no specific amount when it comes to giving an offering, but we are to give offerings as we are led by the Spirit. The Bible says, *"Each man should give what he has decided in his heart to give, not reluctantly or under compulsion, for God loves a cheerful giver"* (2 Corinthians 9:7).

Another important factor we must understand is to whom should our tithe and offering should go towards. The tithe belongs to your local church, where you and your family attend on a regular or weekly basis. It does not belong to the televangelist even though there are preachers on the airwaves today that will tell you to tithe to their ministries. This is neither right nor biblical, however, it is not a problem to give an offering to different ministries around the world. There are good, fruitful, and effective ministries out there that will put your offering to good use, such as feeding the poor and needy, building churches and orphanages, and training up pastors and leaders. We must seek the Lord and pray about this. Talk to your local church pastors or leaders for guidance in this matter.

Let's look at few other examples in Scripture concerning the area of giving:

> *So King Solomon exceeded all the kings of the earth for riches and for wisdom. And all the earth sought to Solomon to hear his wisdom, which God had put in his heart. And they brought every man his present, vessels of silver, and vessels of gold, and garments, and armour, and spices, horses, and mules, a rate year by year.* (1 Kings 10:23-25)

> *And they received of Moses all the offering, which the children of Israel had brought for the work of the service of the sanctuary, to make it withal. And they brought yet unto him free offerings every morning...And they spake unto Moses, saying, The people bring much more than enough for the service of the work, which the Lord commanded to make.* (Exodus 36:3,5)

> *Neither was there any among them that lacked: for as many as were possessors of lands or houses sold them, and brought the prices of the things that were sold. And laid them down at the apostles' feet: and distribution was made unto every man according as he had need. (Acts 4:34,35)*

Health Care

Health and medicine have a long record in human history. It ranges from different medical practices during the times of the Egyptians to the Babylonians. In the time of the Greeks, they took it a step further, introducing the concept of medical diagnosis. During the Medieval Age, surgical practices were inherited from ancient doctors or physicians, then improved and systematized as the years progressed. During the Renaissance Movement, greater understanding of the human anatomy was developed and the microscope was invented. By the mid-twentieth century, great discoveries were being made, such as new biological treatments like antibiotics. The concepts of chemistry, genetics, and different technologies were leading up to modern medicine. Why am I saying all this? We have a supernatural resource available to us in the Kingdom of God. It's called healing. We have already seen in different passages that when Jesus came preaching the Kingdom of God, it was immediately followed by sick people being healed, blind eyes were opened, deaf ears were unstopped, and crippled men and women got up and walked. We also read the accounts of Jesus, where people were being bought back from the dead. In the gospel of Mark it reads:

> *And a certain woman, which had an issue of blood twelve years, and had suffered many things of many physicians, and had spent all that she had, and was nothing bettered, but rather grew worse. When she had heard of Jesus, came in the press behind, and touched his garment. For she said (Matthew says, she said within herself), If I may touch his clothes, I shall be made whole. And straightway the fountain of her blood was dried up, and she felt in her body that she was healed of that plague...And he said unto her, Daughter, thy faith hath made thee whole; go in peace, and be whole of thy plague.* (Mark 5:25-34 Emphasis added)

What am amazing King we serve! It is our right to receive healing. God does not want us to be sick and diseased. The Bible is filled with Scriptures describing God's healing power. Yes, medical technology has its place in our world. Doctors, nurses, and medicine are all necessary and serve a purpose, but there is and always has been a supernatural resource available to everyone at any time. We just need to believe and have faith in God!

It is a ridiculous belief when people believe that sickness and disease came from God to teach them a lesson. This is anti-biblical! It is God's will for every person to be healed and made whole from every sickness and disease! He is Jehovah-Rapha, the God that heals you! All you have to do is call upon Him, your King, and He will answer and restore you to health.

Abiding by the Law

Every kingdom has a set of laws, decrees, and edicts. The king's word becomes law. When laws are declared and established, they become the bedrock of order and justice. We must understand that when laws are established, they are by no means intended to demean the citizen or make their lives more difficult. The purpose of a law is to protect the citizens. We must also understand that no kingdom or government can operate or function without laws. Every kingdom, both past and present, is governed by its laws. It is by these laws that a kingdom can work successfully and peacefully. If we are not careful to abide by these laws, we risk the penalty of imprisonment and even death.

Listen to what the Psalmist said, *"The law of the Lord is perfect, converting the soul: the testimony of the Lord is sure, making wise the simple...Moreover, by them is thy servant warned: and in keeping of them there is great reward"* (Psalm 19:7,11). Every person should feel a sense of enlightenment and joy in keeping the law, whether they be the laws of the land, or God's laws. Can you imagine if every person on this earth did what they felt was right in their own eyes? We see this portrayed in the children of Israel in Scripture. In the Old Testament, it was written many times, *"The children of Israel did what was right in their own eyes."* What if every person on the planet did what was right in his own eyes? There would be chaos and disorder. However, we must be careful when we obey the law because there is not always going to be a reward. Why? When we choose to obey the speed limit within the city, the mayor or police commissioner is not going to visit our houses with a reward for keeping the speed limit. We must be willing, as citizens of the kingdom, to obey every law of the kingdom because we know it's right, whether we receive a reward or not. This is how we show honour to the king and the laws of the land.

We have to understand that there is a penalty for breaking the law. In our modern society, we have a justice system, directed at upholding social control, deterring and mitigating crime, and sanctioning those who violate laws with criminal penalties and rehabilitation efforts. This is carried out through authorized and appointed personnel, who are police officers and judges.

We must understand that God has a set of laws, and if we break those laws, we are guilty and deserve punishment. There is much debate in many Christian circles today about this topic. Many Christians and ministry organizations believe that we don't live under the law of Moses anymore, but under grace, which is correct. However, these same people have done away completely with the law of God as written in the law of Moses. They have the excuse that we are living in the New Testament and in a time of grace. Jesus and Paul debated this with their audiences in their lifetime. Paul said, *"We are no longer under the law but under grace"* (Romans 6:14)! However, he expressively said, *"What then? Shall we continue in sin because we are no longer law but under grace? By no means"* (Romans 6:15)! In the Judicial system, there is a slight possibility that the judge and jury may drop the charges against the defendant. We call this a second chance. However, this same individual is given the opportunity to make a better life for himself under a watchful eye and is scrutinized regularly. If he commits another criminal offence, he will be judged once again and likely be incarcerated for his actions and failure to show any improvement in his life.

Thank God for His mercy and grace, but we must continually be watchful of the things and thoughts around us. We live in a world of temptation, and there are things that are going to try and gain our attention. This is all part of the Kingdom of God. Who is sitting on the throne of our hearts? Is it God, or is it us? Is it the things we enjoy and take pleasure in? In the First Epistle of John, it says,

> *Everyone who sins breaks the law; in fact, sin is lawlessness. But you know that when he appeared so that he might take away our sins. And in him is no sin. No one who lives in him keeps on sinning. No one who continues in sin has neither seen him or known him.* (1 John 3:4-6)

John the Baptist, speaking with the religious leaders of his day, gave this warning, *"Produce fruit in keeping with repentance...and every tree that does not produce good fruit will be cut down and thrown into the fire*" (Matthew 3:8-10). What do you think will happen to us if we keep on sinning? What do you think the penalty will be? Will we be cut off from grace? I challenge and encouragement you to live in accordance with God's Word, His laws and ways, and continually strive to live a life that is pleasing in God's eyes. We can see this in the life of Job. God Himself boasted about this man. The Bible says of Job, "*...was blameless and upright; he feared God and shunned evil...there is no one on earth like him*" (Job 1:1,8). When we look at the life of Job and others in the Bible, we tend to think we should live our Christian lives avoiding sin or the appearance of sin. We shun everything in and around us so that our Christian life becomes a life of just continually avoiding things. Remember this statement: Christianity is not doing, but becoming! We must continue to strive to become more Christ-like in this present world. Yes, there are things that we must avoid and not associate ourselves with, but that must not be our focus.

Our entire world is governed by laws and without them, there would be chaos. For instance, let's take the law of gravity. If we walk too close to the edge of a high building or tower we are going to fall because the law of gravity causes us to fall, which will result in us getting hurt or even dying. Everything in our entire universe is governed by laws. There is the law of reproduction. If they so choose to follow the laws of nature, they will multiply and flourish. Fish are designed to live and breathe underwater, because its all part of natural law. If they choose not to, they will suffocate and die. This is natural law.

During the temptation of Jesus in the wilderness, He said to Satan, who was tempting Him, "*Man shall not live by bread alone, but by every word that comes from the mouth of God*" (Matthew 4:4)! We have read in the Bible that the law of God is perfect. This is not simply God's way of keeping us under submission so that we cannot enjoy life; but those laws have been put in place to protect and sustain us. We must remember we are citizens in covenant with the King and His Kingdom. In every kingdom, the law is established and when kept, protects the citizens and preserves the kingdom so that everyone in that kingdom can enjoy the peace and privileges it offers. But it is not enough to just know the laws of the kingdom; they must be lived out and obeyed. We have been given keys to the Kingdom. Jesus was speaking to Peter when He said, *"And I will give unto thee the keys of the kingdom of heaven..."* (Matthew 16:19). In other words, Jesus was giving Peter responsibilities. Remember, in this section, we are talking about rights and responsibilities. It is our responsibility to keep the law and preserve it.

> *The law of thy mouth is better than thousands of gold and silver.* (Psalm 119:72)

These are excellent benefits that we can and should receive from the King and His Kingdom. This is all part of seeking His kingdom, which we will discuss later.

Our Citizenship – in Heaven?

Paul made an interesting statement in his Epistle to the church in Philippi. The *King James Version* of the Bible uses the word, *conversation,* however, the *New International Version* gives us a more accurate translation and uses the word, *citizenship.*

> *But our citizenship is in heaven. And we eagerly await a Saviour from there, the Lord Jesus Christ, who, by the power that enables him to bring everything under his control, will transform our lowly bodies so that they will be like his glorious body.* (Philippians 3:20)

Early in this chapter we spoke about citizenship. In Paul's day, the citizens of Philippi were also citizens of Rome, and therefore, were able to partake in all the rights and privileges of Rome, yet they had never been to Rome! A majority of the people living in Philippi knew very well that they were citizens even though they were not living there.

N.T. Wright, in his book *Surprised by Hope,* said,

> *When Paul says, "We are citizens of heaven" he doesn't at all mean that when we're done with this life, we'll be going*

off to live in paradise. What he means is that the Saviour, the Lord, Jesus the King — all of those were, of course, imperial titles — will come from heaven to earth, to change the present situation and state of His people. The key word is transform: He will change our current humble bodies to be like His glorious body.

Wright also explains in his book, *The Resurrection of the Sons of God,*

Paul knew...that Roman citizenship (the obvious model behind this imagery) created neither an expectation that one would make the city's one's eventual home. The point about citizenship is a point about status and allegiance, not place of residence. Indeed, the colonists of Philippi a century before Paul's day had been placed there precisely because nobody wanted them back in Rome, or even Italy; there was too much overcrowding, unemployment, and shortage of food in Rome as it was... [The Roman citizen's] task was to live in the colony by the rules of the mother city, not to yearn to go home again.

In this case, it was in the best interest of Rome to expect every citizen to spread the influence of the homeland. Their expectation of every citizen was to bring the culture of Rome to Philippi, therefore when the Roman Emperor or Caesar visited, he would feel right at home.

Philippi had become an extension of the Roman Empire, with many retired Roman soldiers settling there. Most of them were encouraged to establish farms and businesses of their own. What was Paul trying to emphasize to the church in Philippi? Although we are considered citizens of heaven, it does not necessarily mean we will go there. This, in fact, meant that you only had the privileges of imperial citizenship; it did not mean that you owned a home in Rome or that you were ever expected to settle there. This may be hard to accept but again, this is all about kingdom expansion, and yes, I believe in a place called heaven, but my challenge to you today is to not be so caught up with the idea of going to heaven that we forget out earthly responsibilities. What is our responsibility? We have a responsibility, as Christ's ambassadors and representatives, to establish and expand the Kingdom of God here on Earth. The key word is transformation. I don't want you to misunderstand my saying that we are not going to heaven. But as we look at the context and history behind what is being said, particularly in Jesus' sayings and Paul's writings, we miss the intention and meaning. This is not a debate about eschatology and the end times, but it changes our perspective and insight towards the Kingdom of God. It is not my intention to destroy a hope in a future place, but to restore a hope in a present reality.

Gnosticism

If we are in touch with church history, we will begin to see that much of these ideas were birthed from Gnosticism. These Gnostics believed, that physical matter is intrinsically corrupt and evil and that the human is a cage imprisoning the heavenly spiritual essence of a person. The good news the Gnostics taught was that if a person believed the correct things, his soul could be set free and then return to its heavenly source, free from the taint of the physical world forever more. Much of these beliefs that these Gnostics engaged themselves in were very much contrary to Jewish belief. We would be surprised at how much our current belief system is based primarily upon Gnosticism. If this is our current thinking and idea of Christianity, then we are no different from any other religion in the world existing today.

Where Do We Go from Here?

It is unfortunate that much of Christianity has placed such a high emphasis on going to heaven in actuality. Paul was strongly emphasized that death would be the last enemy destroyed, (1 Corinthians 15:26), but today it has become our first and closest option to free us from the wretched state and shackles of this world and release us to our home in heaven. Again, this is not meant to cause confusion, but is simply a vehicle to help us better understand our role and responsibility as Kingdom citizens. The church of Jesus Christ has been so focused on wanting to leave and escape this earth and all of its complications and problems, that, unfortunately, this whole idea has dominated and defined the church in every way. As I shared in the second chapter of this book, our entire focus has been on the great escape from this earth, that we have forgotten our God-given responsibility. Again, I believe in a place called heaven and I believe we will, at some point, be given the option to enter into that place. But our focus should and must be this place called earth. While we still have breath in our lungs, movement in our bodies, and sound in our voices, we should be proclaiming the wonderful news of the Kingdom of God to the world around us. The only question remains: where do we go from here? As I look at church history and the revivals recorded there, I noticed they were centered and focused on the glory of God invading every person, church, and nation! We should be looking for and expecting a heavenly invasion rather than an earthly evacuation, and waiting for a grand entrance rather than a great escape.

CHAPTER 7

Seeking His Kingdom

But seek ye first the kingdom of God, and his righteousness;
and all these things shall be added unto you. (Matthew 6:33)

I wanted to dedicate an entire section to this verse because sometimes we can recite or say a verse without ever knowing what we are saying. We cannot just read one single verse out of context, pray a prayer to God and simply expect Him to bless us in every area of our lives. In the entire chapter of Matthew six, Jesus was probably speaking to a large crowd. He was using the religious leaders as examples of what not to do, something Jesus was in the habit of doing. Here Jesus had no problem with public praying, fasting, or giving, but the problem He was addressing was the intent and motivation of the heart. Jesus had already given them the model prayer earlier in the chapter, in which we are to pray His Kingdom come, and His will be done on earth as it is in heaven. He later began to speak about the prayer of gaining possessions.

God does not have an issue with us wanting and desiring certain things. There was a statement I heard some years ago, *"It's not wrong to have possessions, as long as the possessions don't have you."* Many Christians believe it is wrong to have such possessions like an expensive car, a five or six bedroom home, and beautiful clothes. People complain about ministers on television who have several cars, pool, a six million dollar home, a private plane, and tailored suits, but no one says a thing about Hollywood celebrities who live similar lives. These ministers are accused of manipulating their Christian audience on television into giving large sums of money to their ministries. My only advice is to pray about it and let the Holy Spirit guide you to whom you should give your money too. However, it is not God's will that we live a life of poverty either. It is in God's best interest, and should be ours, that we live a prosperous life and serve as examples to the people around us and the world. One important issue we must address is this – the king's reputation and his kingdom are at stake and when we have this mentality. Craig S. Keener said,

> *In Judaism God was a Father who delighted in meeting the needs of his people; Judaism also recognized that God knew all a person's thoughts. Jesus predicates effective prayer on a relationship of intimacy, not a business partnership model, which was closer to the one followed by ancient paganism.*

The whole idea of seeking was one of intimacy. What does the Bible portray when it uses the word *seek*? How would we define it today? The Bible uses this word *"seek"* throughout Scripture in similar ways. The word *seek* is attached to *the desire to seek, to find* and is used to describe as *one thinking, meditating, and reasoning or enquiring into*. It also describes as *one who aims at, to strive after, to demand, and to crave*. We see that through this simple word, it is not a passive thing, but used aggressively.

Matthew also uses the word, *first*. *"But seek ye first..."* (Matthew 6:33). In other words, it is to be the first and foremost thing we seek after. The Kingdom of God must become the priority in our praying, our giving, our worshiping, and our very lives. In fact, in this same chapter, Jesus taught on the very area of praying, giving, and fasting. He said, *"When you, pray...give...fast."* Notice He did not say, if you pray, give, or fast.

We are living in a world today which seeks after so many things with which to satisfy or relieve our carnal desires. The book of Proverbs says, *"There is a way which seemeth right unto a man, but the end thereof are the ways of death"* (Proverbs 14:12). To our surprise, we are living in a consumer generation. Many people in our world today, desire to have the latest technology. Is this wrong? Absolutely not! But where are our priorities? Jeremiah also declared, *"O Lord, I know that the way of man is not in himself: it is not in man that walketh to direct his paths"* (Jeremiah 10:23). In every area of our lives, we should be seeking after the King and His kingdom. We can easily get caught up in society that we forget that we are children of God and we have the Holy Spirit living inside of us.

His Righteousness

But seek ye first the kingdom of God, and his righteousness...
(Matthew 6:33)

When reading this one verse, many believers stop after *seeking His kingdom*. But what does Jesus mean when He says, *"...and his righteousness"*? Paul said to the church in Corinth, *"For he hath made him to be sin for us, who knew no sin; that we might be made the righteousness of God in him"* (2 Corinthians 5:21). It is ultimately clear that Christ bore our sins on the cross of Calvary. This is a given for us, and we understand this to be true. Paul was saying we have become Christ's righteousness, ambassadors, here on earth as representatives. This entire verse carries within itself the idea of representation which was already set forth when Paul spoke about being an ambassador. In other words, the people in this world will never see Jesus in the flesh, and they can never see Him fully manifested, except through His representatives and ambassadors. That is why it is imperative that we become Christ-like. We are the only Jesus that this world will ever see!

His righteousness signifies the importance of representation. In the previous verse, Paul said, *"Now then we are ambassadors for Christ..."* (2 Corinthians 5:20). An ambassadorial representative is only as viable and legal as his relationship is with the government which he represents. In the beginning, the Bible spoke of the Lord coming down in the cool of the day. It was like the Chairman or President of some corporation coming to check on business. This informs us that God had a long standing relationship with Adam, who was His representative down here on earth. When the Fall of man had taken place, business had been ruined and it turn they were terminated from their authoritative position. But thank God, now we have the Holy Spirit living inside of us and He serves as a voice between us and that heavenly Kingdom to do His will here on Earth.

Aligned through Righteousness

We must take into consideration that *righteousness* is not a religious word. It actually comes from the etymology of law. An interesting word that is attached to righteousness is *alignment*. Righteousness is when we come into alignment with the governing authority of the kingdom. It is necessary that we abide by the laws given in God's Word, as we have seen in chapter six. When we seek the Kingdom of God and His righteousness, we are not only seeking after the Kingdom by making it a priority in our lives, but we are also seeking the governing authority of that Kingdom, therefore aligning and submitting ourselves to its governmental standards and laws. When we are out of alignment, this is where disorder and chaos come in.

A great example of alignment is the tires on our vehicles. When the steering column goes out of alignment, it affects the tire life. This will cause the vehicle's suspension system to be improperly aligned, create uneven tire wear, and a shorter life expectancy. When our tires are not properly aligned, it will pull our vehicles to the left or the right, undermining our control over it while driving. In this, we put other motorists at risk.

This applies to our churches and ministries as well. When we don't align ourselves with the standards and ways of God, we run the risk of wearing out and being pulled to the left or the right in our attempts at Kingdom business and expansion. We must also remember that God is a God or order. Let me impose a question, would you ever use a toilet that has the sign *"Out of Order"* stamped on it? Probably not! Unfortunately, this has been the case with so many churches and ministries. We are ignoring the sign that reads *"Out of Order!"* but are still continuing church as usual. We need an alignment of spiritual things. We need to be set back in order. To do that, we must first seek the Kingdom of God and His righteousness.

What Is Our Focus?

The problem with most Christians and ministries today is we are driving while looking in the rear-view mirror. What does this mean? We can look at the lives of the roaring reformers such as Martin Luther, John Calvin, John Knox, and the revivalists such as John Wesley, George Whitefield, and Jonathan Edwards. We also have powerful, influential men like Charles Finney, Dwight L. Moody, and Evan Roberts. Our Christian heritage is filled with innumerable accounts of great movements of God. Despite all these incredible events in our history, what is our goal? Are we going to continue to look back and only imagine what it might have been like during those times? Are these events that transpired in church history the only source of strength and inspiration we have for today? What has been our focus? What are we seeking after? Yes, we can learn from these great men and women of God in the past, but we shouldn't try to duplicate them and their ministries.

Why are we not seeing more and more people getting healed? Why are we not seeing more people getting saved and set free? Why are our churches being emptied rather than being filled? We have done everything else but seek after His Kingdom and His righteousness. It goes far beyond just believing in the Kingdom. Far more importantly, the Kingdom has been placed in the future for another time and place, so therefore, we cannot operate in that Kingdom power and authority. How can we expect to have more healing, miracles, deliverances, and salvations when the Kingdom of God has been moved to the future? It is time to start seeking after the Kingdom of God and His righteousness today! When we start taking the Kingdom verses from the Bible and applying them to a future time, we are making a lot of Scripture irrelevant to us today. In the book of Matthew alone, there are many references to the Kingdom. We must seek *first* His Kingdom!

I don't know about you, but I am glad to be living in this day and age. We have seen the development and advancement of technology that makes it all the more possible to share the gospel of Jesus Christ around the world. What happened in and through these great men and women of the past, can happen again. So we must learn from their lives, and build strength through the Holy Spirit. We must determine that our lives and ministries will not only make the records of church history, but also be found in the records of heaven. Let us seek wholeheartedly after the Kingdom of God. When He comes with His Kingdom, we will see heaven invade once again, just as in times past.

CHAPTER 8

The Kingdom Now

Throughout this entire discourse, we have discussed several critical issues that are lacking in the church today. Although there may have been some form of what has been presented here today, there exists a void within the Body of Christ that has left us powerless and lifeless.

> *As the rain and the snow come down from heaven, and do not return to it without watering the earth and making it bud and flourish, so that it yields seed for the sower and bread for the eater, so is my word that goes out from my mouth: It will not return to me empty, but will accomplish what I desire and achieve the purpose for which I sent it. (Isaiah 55:10,11)*

There is a Word that is given to humanity and the church. It is the Kingdom of God! We have only begun to see a restoration of this, and we see it emerging in different ministries and churches. What are we afraid of? What if our understanding of the Bible and the way we've believed for so many years crumbles down to ashes because of our new found belief in the Kingdom of God? It is a risk I'm willing to take. God called Jeremiah to a particular task, saying, *"See, I have this day set thee over the nations and over the kingdoms, to root out, and to pull down, and* to destroy, and to throw down, to build, and to plant" (Jeremiah 1:10). In order to build a new world, it usually means having to tear the old one down. When this happens, it creates enemies.

Called as Sons & Daughters

Yet to all who did receive him, to those who believed in his name, he gave the right to become children of God.
(John 1:12)

God has called us to a wonderful plan and purpose. The day we begin to become satisfied will be the day our religious life begins. We must continue to hunger for more every day of our lives. I recall the story of the Prodigal Son, to which most of us can relate. We all know the story. Every so often, too many of God's people get caught up with the idea of being *"workers"* in the field or vineyard, that we forget what it means to be *"sons in the house."* David Ravenhill said,

> *It is a story of God's response to one of His children coming home. It's a story that could be titled, Lost and Found. In the case of unclaimed luggage, it was lost forever. God, however, never gives up on His lost children, no matter how far or how long they may stray from home. Not a day goes by that the Father doesn't longingly and lovingly gaze, waiting patiently for some sign of His returning child. Unlike unclaimed luggage, the Father longs to reclaim every lost child who is willing to acknowledge his need and turn his heart toward Him.*

We are called to be sons and daughters of the Kingdom of God. It is time we take up our rightful place. It is time to silence the naysayers and the doubters. These noises and voices have grown so loud that we can longer hear the voice of the Shepherd calling us out of a life of lethargy and out of the shadows. Rise and take your place as a son and daughter. Steve Gray said,

God is gathering up Kingdom people once more. These are the people distressed with dead religion that has lost the presence of God. They are worn out by indebtedness to sins that they were promised would no longer have power over them. They are discontented by churches with little real interest in the living God and that are filled with division, carnality, and the works of the flesh. They are worn out with self-help and self-improvement preaching while the spiritual condition of the Church declines.

Perhaps you are one of these people sitting in a church pew Sunday after Sunday with little knowledge of God's plan and purpose for your life. Maybe you are just sitting at home wondering when Jesus is going to come back and take us all away. We were never meant or destined to remain idle while on this planet. Maybe you are one of those that have become dissatisfied and discontented with what's going on in the church today. What if I were to tell you that we can hasten the coming of the Lord? The answer may surprise you. God is not holding out on us, we are holding out on Him. He is waiting on us! It is the day of the Kingdom of God.

Roberts Liardon said,

It seems that evangelicalism today has shifted from a spiritual to a political emphasis. While we still largely focus on the work of evangelism, we have laid aside the power of God for the more easily controlled power of a conservative voting block. We seem to have forgotten that it was revivalism that changed nations and righted social injustices during the past three centuries – not the power of democracy or the right to vote alone. It seems that evangelical Christianity has lost much of its relevance to societies because it tends to focus more on changing laws than changing hearts.

God is not going to abandon creation, as many Christians believe. On the contrary, as Romans says, *"We know that the whole creation has been groaning as in the pains of childbirth right up to the present time"* (Romans 8:22). What is creation waiting for? God is simply waiting on ordinary people like you and me. The manifestation of the sons of God. Creation was groaning because it knew what mankind was like since the dawn of Creation. Adam carried the very nature, character, and glory of God. Since that time, and from the time of Noah, creation waits in eager expectation for that same nature and character to be revealed through mankind again. He not only has a plan for us, but He also has a plan and a purpose for this Earth that He created. In fact, this is His investment. What if a realtor decided to abandon and demolish a house after investing millions of dollars into it? That would be terrible business and a waste of money. God is not going to abandon this world as many suppose. In fact, I believe He has a plan and purpose for an entire restoration of this world in which we live in. We are going to see the glory of God cover this world as the waters cover the sea.

What Time is It?

It is up to us to embrace the invitation given by the King Himself and see ourselves in this vital role as in this plan. Maybe it's time to renew your citizenship in the Kingdom. We have been created for so much more than just filling a seat in the church building. We were created to walk in the authority and dominion given by the King.

And I saw heaven opened, and behold a white horse; and he that sat upon him was called Faithful and True, and in righteousness, he doth judge and make war. His eyes were as a flame of fire, and on his head were many crowns; and he had a name written, that no man knew, but he himself. And he was clothed with a vesture dipped in blood: and his name is called The Word of God. And the armies which were in heaven followed him upon white horses, clothed in fine linen, white and clean. And out of his mouth goeth a sharp sword, that with it he should smite the nations: and he shall rule them with a rod of iron: and he treadeth the winepress of the fierceness and wrath of Almighty God. And he hath on his vesture and on his thigh a name written...

KING OF KINGS AND LORD OF LORDS!

(Revelation 19:11-16 Emphasis added)

The King and the Kingdom are here and God wants you to be a part of it!

BIBLIOGRAPHY

Biro, Adam R. A. <u>Kingdom of Priests – Special Treasure Holy Nation Royal Priesthood</u>
Publication of Faith Alive Bible College, Saskatoon, SK., 2014. Print.

DeArteaga, William, <u>Quenching the Spirit: Examining Centuries of Opposition to the Moving of the Holy Spirit</u>, Lakeland, FL: Creation House, 1992

Elwell, A. Walter. <u>Evangelical Dictionary of Biblical Theology</u>
Published by Baker Books, Grand Rapids, MI. 1996.

Gaines, Bertram L. <u>This Gospel of the Kingdom – Accessing the Power for Triumphant Christian Living</u> Destiny Images Publishers, Inc. Shippensburg, PA., 1999. Print.

Gray, Steve <u>Follow the Fire – Personal Renewal Is Just A Decision Away</u>
Published by Charisma House, Lake Mary, FL., 2001. Print.

Gray, Steve <u>My Absurd Religion – By Which I Make My Living</u>
Published by World Revival Press, Kansas City, MO., 2008. Print.

Gray, Steve <u>When the Kingdom Comes – Lessons from the Smithton Outpouring</u>
Published by World Revival Press, Kansas City, MO., 1999. Print.

Keener, Craig S. The IVP Bible Background Commentary – New Testament
InterVarsity Press, Downers Grove, IL, 2000. Print.

King, J.D. Kingdom of God – Correspondence Course
World Revival Church, Kansas City, MO., 2011. Print.

Liardon, Roberts God's Generals – The Revivalists
Whitaker House, New Kensington, PA., 2008. Print.

Morphew, Derek J. Breakthrough – Discovering the Kingdom
Struik Christian Books Ltd., 1991. Print.

Munroe, Myles Rediscovering the Kingdom – Ancient Hope for our 21st Century World
Destiny Images Publishers, Inc. Shippensburg, PA., 2004. Print.

Pfeifer, Mark W. Alignment – A Blueprint for the 21st Century Church
Morris Publishing, Kearney, NE, May 2009. Print.

Ravenhill, David Welcome Home – Based on the Parable of the Prodigal Son
Destiny Image Publishers, Inc. Shippensburg, PA, 2008. Print.

Ravenhill, Leonard Why Revival Tarries – A Classic On Revival
Bethany House Publishers, Minneapolis, MN., 1959. Print.

Walton, John H., Matthew, Victor H., Chavalas, Mark W. The IVP Bible Background Commentary – Old Testament
InterVarsity Press, Downers Grove, IL., 2000. Print.

Welton, Jonathan Raptureless: An Optimistic Guide to the End of the World
Amazon, Kindle e-books. 2013. Print.

Wright, N. T. <u>Surprised by Hope – Rethinking Heaven, the Resurrection, and the Mission of the Church</u>
HarperCollins e-books. 2008. Print.

Wright, N. T. <u>The Resurrection of the Sons of God</u>
HarperCollins e-books. 2008. Print.

ABOUT THE AUTHOR

Alec was raised on a small First Nation reservation in northwestern Ontario. After accepting Jesus Christ as Lord and Savior of his life, he endeavored to serve God wholeheartedly. He is a graduate from Bible College, earning a Diploma in Theology. After some years in ministry, he continued his studies and obtained a Bachelor's and Master's Degree in Theology. He is currently in the process of completing his Doctorate Degree. Alec has served both in evangelistic and pastoral ministry for many years. His passion for preaching and teaching has taken him across northern Canada. Alec has a desire for training and discipleship, and a deep desire for ministers to be well equipped. He and his wife, Kareen, and their son, Landon, now reside in Saskatoon, Saskatchewan.

For additional copies or more information about the author:
Email: ancapay@gmail.com
(Email is for ordering and ministry purposes only)